THE ANONYMOUS LANDLORD

ISBN: 9798386323233

IMPRINT: Independently published

Copyright 2023, Tom Soane

This book was produced in collaboration with Write Business Results Limited. For more information on their business book and marketing services, please visit www.writebusinessresults.com or contact the team via info@writebusinessresults.com.

 WRITE BUSINESS RESULTS

THE ANONYMOUS LANDLORD

Make profit from property without sacrificing time, energy, family and mind

Tom Soane

ACKNOWLEDGEMENTS

My mum is my inspiration, my idol and my rock. She was relentless in her pursuit of success and kept my life full of fun and happiness no matter what shit she was going through herself – even when we were practically homeless, having nearly lost our home, and had nothing at all. We still had fun and made the most of every day in every part of life. My mother taught dancing in her own business but, more importantly, she taught people how to achieve their own dreams. It was the same for me.

It was her support and attitude that gave me my relentless ambition and drive. Although she didn't make her business into any sort of money-making machine, she's helped hundreds of children achieve their dreams in performing arts. I get my natural desire to help and educate people from my mum. I get my desire to make the most of all parts of life from my mum. And I get my business brain from my mum.

She won't understand that, but I watched her struggle in her business, watched her fail, succeed, cry, laugh. I watched her try to take everything on herself and get very little financial return from her money, time and energy investments. She worked so hard every single day; she was relentless and never stopped putting effort into building her dream into a reality. But I also watched her constantly learn and develop herself – to always improve, always adapt.

I must have put all that together and subconsciously made the decision NOT to do it all myself and to instead focus on my strengths so that I could make the most of life and my successes. Our holidays were in a second-hand tent in the middle of a field through storms while my friends went abroad every year! Our car was a £100 Lada Select. Our house was full of charity shop items – I didn't care or realise, I was so happy. Mum, I love you and thank you for everything you've sacrificed and endured to give me the most incredible life!

My dad always taught me to surround myself with good people who can do the things I can't; he showed me if I surround myself with the right people I'll never struggle in life. This has proven to be instrumental in building my businesses.

My stepdad taught me not only to work hard, but he also said, "If you're going to do a job, you might as well do it to the best of your ability." He put up with a lot from me and never left my side.

My wife is my best friend, my partner in life, my supporter. She's building her own business now and I could not be prouder. She's been with me through good times and terrible times in my business – from bailiffs banging my door down every day and losing everything – my house, my car, my business – to now, where we're financially secure, stable and free. All the way, she showed me the same love and support that my mum did when she was struggling. We still made the most of life. We still made sure we kept working our arses off to achieve the dreams we knew we could achieve.

Sally Lawson, my mentor. I started working with Sally when I was almost ready to quit in business. Sally helped me bring out my potential, showed me how to use my strengths to build a fantastic business and brought my creative business brain into action. Sally is a real inspiration to anybody who is in need of direction. I owe her so much.

David Pike, a friend of the family and a successful businessman. He said one thing to me which started my journey to success (which I'm not at yet but well on my way). I sat with David and poured out my business problems. "It's my baby," I said. "I've poured my blood, sweat and tears into this business." To which he looked at me, puzzled, and said one of the greatest business quotes I've heard ... "Tom, your business is not your baby. Your business is nothing more than a vehicle which is designed specifically to generate money, that's it."

Luke Tilley, a friend and property investor. Luke gave me a priceless quote which really detached me from my business enabling me to see it for what it is rather than getting consumed by the emotions, fears and ego involved. During a challenging property purchase, Luke said to me, "Tom, it's just a pile of bricks." BAM! That hit me hard and my logical property brain took over.

Leigh Medway, for coming back! For always believing in me and always having my back. Leigh worked for me during times where I couldn't afford to pay staff, bills, rent, or anything else. She stuck with me knowing I was destined to succeed. Leigh gives me (and everyone around her) an unbreakable belief in themselves, just like my mum. Thanks for everything you do, Leigh.

Peter Appleton. He'll never read this! He doesn't read books because, in his words, "Why would I read books? I've got the internet." Pete changed my life. I won't go into detail, but Pete helped me get to where I am now and he's helped me develop my business brain, my way of thinking, and my attitude towards business.

Jody Gough. Without Jody I wouldn't have started in business all those years ago. While we might not be the same in business now, we had so much fun back then. Jody has been my brother since we were kids. We have been inseparable ever since and now we're grown ups, I look back at that time knowing that I owe him for giving me the confidence to take the plunge into business.

My kids, Harrison and Mason. You are the reason I do everything. Every decision I make, every pound I invest, every improvement I make, it's all for you, boys.

TO MY SONS, MY WORLD, MY LIFE

Be kind and honest with everyone,
Listen to everyone, learn everything.
Go for it! Never stop going for it,
Feel the fear, and do it anyway.
Don't take shit, don't give any shit,
Grow your money and keep it safe,
Always invest, always make profit.
Be active, competitive, try your best,
Look after your body, eat well, train,
Practise, practise, practise, play,
Be the best you can be in all you do.
Keep growing, improving yourself,
Be a better version of you every day,
You can't fail if you learn and adapt,
You only fail when you quit.
Life is awesome, make the most of it,
Have fun, laugh, smile, and enjoy it.
Watch *Star Wars* in order of release,
Look after your mum, she's amazing!
Always make time for a daddy cuddle.
I love you, I'm proud of you,
I love being your dad,
I'm with you forever.

DEDICATION

I want to dedicate this to everyone who owns a property as an investment – traditional landlords, accidental landlords, new landlords, future landlords. At some point in your lives, whether you believe it or not, you made an investment decision to invest in a property or to keep a property you could have sold. It could be for your children's futures, your own future, your own cash flow – anything. Whatever your reason for becoming an investor-landlord, let's turn it into a business that runs and grows without you.

CONTENTS

FOREWORD

by Paul Shamplina

I've been acting for landlords for over 30 years, have worked with thousands of letting agents across the country and I can tell you that being a landlord now is harder and riskier than it's ever been. Period.

There's more legislation around being a landlord than there ever has been before. On the horizon, as I write this, is the Renters' Reform Bill, the abolition of Section 21, the end of fixed-term tenancies, and the EPC upgrades that will be required as part of the Green Deal. Alongside an increase in legislation is an increase in costs for landlords, with Section 24 causing many landlords to pay more tax – which presents another big challenge.

The only way you are going to overcome these challenges is to have the right people and suppliers, with the right knowledge, around you. Regardless of how many properties you own, you need to think like a professional landlord, which is precisely what this book will teach you.

At Landlord Action, we are seeing record numbers of landlords leaving the sector, but this in itself creates opportunities. Demand for rental properties is at the highest it's ever been. This means landlords have a far better pool of tenants applying to rent their properties than ever before. What's more, those tenants are bidding against one another for these properties, which means landlords are also receiving more rent than ever before.

Many DIY landlords won't capitalise on this though because they don't have the support in place to do so. Many don't even realise everything they need to do to comply with current legislation as a landlord, let alone any new legislation that is coming their way in the future.

The best piece of advice I can give you is to find a letting agent. I work with letting agents around the country and I know Tom goes into how to find the right letting agent to support you in great detail in this book.

Too many DIY landlords see a letting agent as a cost, but when you add up all the hours you spend managing your rental properties – not to mention all the risks of being a DIY landlord, as well as all the lost money, time spent, increased stress, hassle, and responsibility – and compare that to a letting agent's monthly fee, you'll realise the value they bring. Not to mention the letting agent keeping your rent at market value for you, which most DIY landlords don't do.

What Tom sets out in this book is what you need to know to survive and thrive as a landlord in today's world. Things are changing faster than ever before in the private rented sector (PRS), which is scary for some landlords. These are the ones who are selling their properties and leaving landlording behind.

But for those who focus on the long term, there are huge opportunities. Not only are there more tenants than ever looking for rental properties, but these tenants are prepared to pay well for a good property owned and managed by a good landlord.

Anonymous landlords are good landlords, because they have the support network in place to not only support themselves but also their tenants.

Remember – your tenant is your customer. Without them none of us would be here. Treat them well and the rest will fall into place.

Paul Shamplina

Founder of Landlord Action and Chief Commercial Officer at Hamilton Fraser

Star of Nightmare Tenants, Slum Landlords

paulshamplina.tv

INTRODUCTION

Are you a landlord who's feeling the pressure and stress because you're spending more time than you'd like managing your rental properties and your tenants? Or are you considering becoming a landlord and want to make sure that you're getting everything right once you have property investments? Either way, this is the book for you. What I'm going to share in the coming chapters is how you can build a successful property investment business, one that works for you, without you, and allows you to generate a predictable, reliable and almost effortless stream of income. This is what it means to be an anonymous landlord.

I can tell you now that what you read in the following pages isn't going to tell you anything unbelievable or shocking. There are no hidden secrets or magical revelations about property investing. The truth, as in most cases, is that you are probably aware of most of what I'm going to cover here but my hope is that I'll be able to give you a new perspective on the world of property investing and landlording. I want to give you a new way to think about being an investor landlord, a way that helps you transform your mindset into that of an anonymous landlord.

What I'll share is what I've learned in my years as a property investor, landlord and owner of a chain of lettings management agencies. The examples I'll share are from everything I've experienced as a property investor and anonymous landlord myself, as well as from managing hundreds of landlords and thousands of tenancies over the last two decades.

None of this is revolutionary, but changing your mindset and perspective around the basics of owning and running your rental properties in the right way can act as a catalyst that propels you towards your dream life and that helps you achieve whatever goals you set for yourself – whether that's cash flow income, growth in property value and equity, portfolio building, financial security for your family, building assets, providing financial wealth for your children, and so on.

I believe that everyone has the potential to be an anonymous landlord, as long as their mindset is in the right place. I'll explain what this mindset is in much more detail in Chapter 2, but in essence this involves shifting from thinking like a traditional landlord, where they have to do everything themselves, to thinking like a modern investor landlord, who relinquishes all or some of the control of the day-to-day in favour of running their property investments like a business.

Traditional landlords will need to transition to this new breed if they are to survive and continue to make money from their property investments due to ever-changing legislation, and the mountain of reforms to regulations that are being proposed for the private rented sector (PRS) in the UK over the coming years.

Over time, traditional landlords are going to be phased out of the market and replaced by investor landlords and anonymous landlords who have set up the right structures to properly manage their properties and tenancies compliantly and in good practice. If you are currently a traditional landlord, this will require you to change your mindset so that you can not only survive, but build a thriving property investment business. It doesn't matter whether you have only one property or 100 properties, the mindset should still be the same.

I'm talking about thinking of your tenants as customers, your properties as products and your management of those properties as the valuable service you (or your team once you become a true anonymous landlord) provide for your tenants. I'll explain this in more detail later on because this is the beginning of the anonymous landlord mindset. It's also vital to your success in property, no matter what your strategy is. Remember that rule: the tenant is the customer, the property is the product and the tenancy management is the service.

Your mindset really is crucial to making this transition, that's why I want to give you a completely new way of looking at your property investments, as well as a different perspective on how you can really succeed in property, so we'll explore this in detail in Part 1. In Part 2, I'll cover the fundamentals of being an anonymous landlord, ranging from finding the right properties to invest in and performing the appropriate due diligence, to how to finance your property investments and how to add value to those properties.

In Part 3, I'll cover what (and who) you need to have in place in order to become a true anonymous landlord and have a successful property investment business that runs without you. I'll also dive into some of the most common challenges landlords face and explain what solutions I've found that have worked for me and for the hundreds of landlords and property investors I've worked with.

But before we get into all of that, let's begin by examining the opportunity that property investment presents to you. And how, with the right perspective and mindset, you can use it to achieve your goals in life.

PART 1:
THE OPPORTUNITIES FOR AN ANONYMOUS LANDLORD

Investing in property is often promoted as a great way to generate a "passive income" or to help you work towards "financial freedom". However, what is often missing from these conversations is what's involved in allowing you to reach the stage where you are spending very little time managing the properties you rent out. That's the dream, right? To generate "passive income". Because nobody invests in property so they can work MORE, right?

Let's be honest, becoming an anonymous landlord takes time and effort, and it won't happen overnight, but it is definitely possible and the rewards you'll get from becoming one are massive. In this first part of the book I'm going to start by talking you through the various ways in which you can profit from property – and it's not all about the financial profit. There are a few different forms of profit to think about.

This is one of the most common mistakes I see landlords making, so I want to help you see your property investments in a different light, which will set you on the path towards becoming an anonymous landlord.

Mindset is absolutely key and, in fact, provides a strong foundation for any anonymous landlord. This isn't going to be a therapy session or a psychology class. The anonymous landlord mindset is a new way of thinking about property – a different perspective and a mindset that will promote success in all areas of your life. You can even take the anonymous landlord mindset into business, life and work.

In Chapter 2 I'll talk to you about what the anonymous landlord mindset is, and share some advice on how you can shift your mindset in this direction. A lot of what I share isn't rocket science, but sometimes you just need someone to help you see things from a different perspective. I remember reading *Rich Dad Poor Dad* by Robert Kiyosaki which completely changed the way I viewed income, expenditure, assets and liabilities. It's the same here. It's a new way of seeing an old thing.

By the end of this part of the book, I'd like you to be thinking of your property investment as a business – I believe property is the easiest business in the world (I'll explain exactly why in Chapter 2), but to really grab all the opportunities it presents, you need to think like an anonymous landlord.

So, let's start by exploring the various pots of profit that exist in property investing, and how you can make sure you're topping all of them up, rather than filling just one of them at the expense of the others.

1 THE PROFIT OF PROPERTY

The phone rings just as Drew is about to sit down to dinner with his family. Beth shoots him a mock look of disapproval as he goes to pick it up – "I'll make it quick, I promise," he says as he answers the phone and walks out of the kitchen.

"Hello ..."

"Hi, it's Lara, from number 62? I'm sorry to call you at this time of the evening, but I didn't think this could wait. The boiler has stopped working and, I mean, it's December and it's freezing out, so we can't really do without heating and hot water ..." she tails off.

"No, no, of course not!" Drew checks himself, he was about to tell Lara he'd get on the case after dinner, but that seems insensitive. "Let me make some calls – I'll get someone out to look at it tonight. I'll call you with an update as soon as I can."

"Thank you, really appreciate it. We'll just wrap up for the time being!" Lara says. Drew sighs as he hangs up the phone. He returns to the kitchen, explains the situation and tells Beth and the kids he'll eat in the office so he can Google emergency heating engineers, thinking to himself, of course this would happen two weeks before Christmas!

Almost an hour and multiple phone calls later, Drew has a heating engineer on the way over to number 62. He's told Lara he'll be there too, which means he's forgoing his evening of reading the kids their bedtime story. Somewhat wearily, Drew heads for the door, grabbing his coat, scarf and gloves as he goes. "Not sure what time I'll be home, just need to get this sorted for Lara and her family," he calls to Beth as he's leaving. "Okay!" is her reply from the children's room where she's taken over storytime. He glances at the clock, it's 8:10pm.

When Drew arrives at Lara's house, it's not much warmer inside than it is out. Her kids are huddled under blankets on the sofa, with a few hot water bottles between them. It looks like she's wearing multiple jumpers under her coat. "Thanks for coming out tonight," she offers. "Not at all, just part of being a landlord!" is Drew's almost automatic response. The heating engineer mercifully arrives within 15 minutes of Drew making it to number 62, but it's not long before he's delivering bad news – namely that the cost of repairs is almost as much as a new boiler. Drew purses his lips, whistling slightly and inwardly wincing at the expense. "Is there anything you can do to get it working for tonight, or at least the next couple of days?" He asks hopefully. "No can do! Sorry, the part will take a week to arrive – you'll do better to just replace it." Drew pauses, "And when could you come to fit a new boiler?" "Earliest I could squeeze it in would be a week Thursday. Sorry mate, it's a busy time of year and what with Christmas coming up ..."

"But that's over a week away!" Drew says, all the heating engineer can do is shrug. He looks over his shoulder to where Lara is sitting on the sofa with her two kids and beckons her over. She looks hopeful, "Can he fix it?" "Well, no, not tonight, I'm really sorry." "But it's freezing! Me and the kids can't all sleep on the sofa." "No, no, of course not. Look, it's probably going to take a week or so to get a new boiler fitted, so I'm going to buy you some electric heaters to keep you all warm until this is fixed. Is that OK?" Drew shakes his head as Lara walks off, clearly not overly happy with the solution.

"Rental property?" The heating engineer asks. Drew just nods. "Look, I'll book this place in for next Thursday, and if any of my other jobs cancel, you'll be the first one I call," he offers. "Thanks, appreciate it," Drew replies.

As Drew walks through the front door he catches sight of the clock, 11:07pm. What a night. On the drive home, he is running through rough calculations of not only the cost of a new boiler, but also the expense of four new electric heaters.

****

Beth is curled up on the sofa, "Take it that wasn't an easy fix?" She inquires. "You could say that," Drew replies, outlining what's happened and watching Beth's face sink as he does, silently cursing the broken boiler and wishing he wasn't a landlord at all at this moment in time.

Does that story sound familiar? Maybe you've experienced something similar, or maybe you're due to experience it in the future. Maybe it wasn't a broken boiler when it happened at one of your rental properties. It could have been a burst pipe and an emergency plumber; a blown appliance and an emergency electrician; a leaking roof and an emergency roofer. Maybe it was something even more catastrophic. When you're a landlord who takes on the running of your property (or properties) yourself, you have to be prepared for phone calls any day, any time, reporting a problem. It is, after all, your job as a landlord to fix these issues for your tenants. But let me ask you this: did you really invest in rental properties so that you could make being a landlord "a job"? Did you invest in property so you could become a tenancy manager, a letting agent or an administrator (or all three)?

I'm willing to bet that you didn't. You invested in property to make a profit, give yourself more financial stability and to build financial independence and a more comfortable life for you and your family. However, the challenge you face is that you feel as though you need to be the person who does all of those jobs in order to make that profit. This is one of the biggest mindset mistakes I see landlords making, and when you think like that you'll never become an anonymous landlord.

Of course, becoming an anonymous landlord is what you're aiming for, it's why you started investing in property and it's why you're reading this book. By the way, whether you consider yourself to be an "accidental landlord" or you purposefully invested in property, you're a property investor. At some point in your life you've made a decision to keep a property as an investment instead of sell. Or you've decided to put your cash towards investing in a property. Believe it or not, any of those scenarios mean you're a property investor.

Instead of doing everything yourself, you have to think of the different pots of profit you have for your investment. These pots are your money pot, your time pot, your energy pot, your mind (mental health) pot and your family pot. If filling up your money pot means you are taking away from your time, energy and family pots, you have to question whether that is worth it.

Look at the story I shared at the beginning of this chapter – Drew is sacrificing time with his family, as well as his own time and energy, to sort an issue for his tenants. In his mind, he's probably "saving" the expense of a letting agent, but what toll will that take in the long run?

Here's the thing – even if doing all this yourself does mean your money pot grows (and it won't always!) what's the point if your other pots are almost empty? I promise you this, when you reach the end of your time on this earth, you aren't going to wish you'd spent more time "working" or doing a "job" that you hadn't intended to do in the first place. You're going to wish you'd spent more time with your children, your mum, your dad, your nan, your family, your friends ... yourself!

As soon as you start breaking the profit of property down in this way, your mindset starts to shift. Whether you're an accidental landlord or an intentional landlord, ask yourself what your intention was when you invested in property. In my experience, most people invest in property (or any other asset for that matter) with the intention of filling up their money pot so that they can work less and therefore gain more in their time, energy, mind, and family and friends pots too.

Most of the property investors I speak to chose to go down this route because they had a vision of owning property that would produce an income and, in doing so, reduce their stress, reduce the amount they have to work and ensure that their family is comfortable and their financial future is secure. That's the *vision* for property investing, and the vast majority of people set out with the right objectives and a focus on all of their pots of profit, because that's what you should be aiming for!

That's why I started property investing. I wanted to build a portfolio for my kids that would generate cash flow as well as grow in value. I still invest in property with the same goal and I ask myself "is this good for my kids?" with every property I look at. That's a great motivator and a great way to analyse a property investment.

However, once you own a property and money comes into the equation, it's easy for your perspective to change and the blinding desire for money to take over from the initial logical strategy that you started with. Instead of thinking about all your pots of profit, your focus becomes very narrow and zooms in on your money pot. You decide you'd rather do everything yourself and make an extra £50 a month or spend more time trying to save £10 here, or £20 there. It might seem logical but it's not.

This decision means your mindset has shifted and that's how you end up becoming a tenancy manager, letting agent, problem solver, contracts manager and administrator. That's how you get into the "job" of property investing that you never really intended to take on. That's how you never really seem to reach that initial goal of working less and making more money. Does that sound familiar? It will feel like you're making more profit but at what cost? Plus, in reality you don't actually make more profit. In fact, you lose profit! I'll explain more about this in a bit.

THE PITFALLS OF THE DIY (SELF-MANAGING) LANDLORD APPROACH

It might surprise you to learn that just 18 per cent of landlords in the UK have their properties managed for them by an agent, so a staggering 82 per cent manage their properties themselves. What's more, only just over half of landlords (around 54 per cent) are compliant with all the legislation and regulations surrounding the private rented sector in the UK, largely because these are frequently being updated and landlords have an increasing level of responsibility for the state of their properties and the homes they're providing for their tenants[1]. Most landlords don't even realise they're non-compliant, that's the most worrying thing.

At the time of writing in 2022, there are around 170 pieces of legislation that landlords have to know about and adhere to. In addition, the penalties for failing to comply with all of this legislation can be heavy, and tenants are now allowed to take landlords directly to court for failing to comply with all the regulations. This means you're potentially running a big risk if you manage your properties yourself, and you may not even realise it.

The reality is that the vast majority of landlords are good people who don't intend to fall short of their regulatory responsibilities, but the problem is that you often don't know what you don't know until it's too late, and

---

1 Department for Levelling Up, Housing & Communities, (2022), *A Fairer Private Rented Sector*, June, available at: https://assets.publishing.service.gov.uk/government/uploads/system/uploads/attachment_data/file/1083378/A_fairer_private_rented_sector_web_accessible.pdf

ignorance of the rules is no defence. There are also landlords who are simply complacent and don't think this is something they need to worry about. Finally, you have a minority who are criminal landlords, which means they know about all the rules and regulations but choose not to follow them.

In my experience, too many landlords think that they need to do everything themselves, and that this is just part and parcel of property investing. They fall into the trap of thinking, because their tenants aren't having issues now (and haven't been much trouble so far) that it's worth doing everything themselves and that the odd issue isn't a big deal. The problem with this attitude is that you have to react to any issues your tenants have, day or night, any day of the year. This is probably costing you money too. More on that later.

You could be in the middle of Christmas dinner only to receive a phone call from your tenant telling you that they have no electricity, no hot water, or a leak and you're legally obliged to react and fix that problem there and then. You can't tell them you'll get to it on 27th December. As we saw with Drew at the start of the chapter, you may have to pay to put your tenant in a hotel or purchase backup items until the issue with their home is resolved. All of this adds up and eats into the profit you have been making.

When you manage properties in this way, you typically don't have the network of support you need to fix issues quickly and smoothly either. Putting the right management setup in place is something I'll talk about in detail later in this book, because it is one of the keys to becoming a successful anonymous landlord.

KNOW THE RISKS

When you're making a choice about whether to manage rental properties yourself, it's vital that you understand the risk you're undertaking in doing so. As I've said, the majority of people who get into property investing do so because they want a low-risk, profitable investment and they believe property is the best route to go down because it can offer an income as well as growth in value. Perfect!

However, by choosing to take on the running of that property or properties yourself, you are turning a low-risk investment into a high-risk one, because of the legislation, regulations and other compliance you have to follow as a landlord. The average fine for non-compliant landlords varies from city to city, but it is always in the thousands (in some locations in the tens of thousands). In fact, the financial risk is higher than ever, because councils have the funding and infrastructure in place to go after "rogue landlords". That phrase simply means non-compliant landlords. Councils will not only fine landlords who are willfully non-compliant, but also those who don't know what they don't know.

Councils are now able to keep these fines as a revenue stream so many are setting up task forces to target non-compliant landlords and any landlords that are not in "good practice". Where focus goes, money flows! And you can be sure that the councils will chase additional revenue with conviction, given the financial challenges many of them face.

Local authorities in the UK are actively working to improve housing standards, which means they are focusing on rental properties in the private rented sector and therefore that your risk of being fined for being non-compliant has increased dramatically in recent years. By choosing to manage your property yourself, you are increasing your risk of being hit with a fine, and in doing so are taking your low-risk property investment into medium or even high-risk territory.

It's not only about potentially falling foul of the law either. Many DIY landlords don't make as much profit as they could from their properties because they don't charge optimal market value rent, and they aren't optimising their income and expenditure either. They're not treating property investing like a business, which often means they're also not paying the right tax. A lot of self-managing landlords will be paying more tax than they're required to because they're not running their property or properties like a business.

The message I'd like you to understand is that if you are managing your rental properties yourself you are more than likely increasing the risk to your investment, and you are likely not making as much profit as you could.

All of this means you're risking many of the pots of profit I talked about at the start of this chapter – your money pot, your time pot, your energy pot, your mind pot, your family pot. This goes against the reasons you got into property investment in the first place; namely to increase your financial stability, reduce your stress and give yourself more time and energy to spend with your family and friends. Or at least, less time working.

I'm not saying you can't manage your properties yourself, quite the opposite in fact. My point is that you need to change the way you think about it. You need to set the right operation in place so that your properties run and make profit in all your profit pots without you.

YOUR VISION FOR PROPERTY INVESTING VS. YOUR LIFE AS A LANDLORD

When you started out on your property investment journey, I expect you wanted to be an anonymous landlord. If you think back to why you invested in property in the first place, it was likely to make some profit, probably in the form of cash flow, each month. You were probably also looking for a "safe" investment vehicle in which to put your money for the longer term, whether that was to help fund your retirement or to provide for your family in the future. Buzzwords like "passive income" and "financial freedom" often get thrown around, and these are often also part of new property investors' visions.

Was this your vision for property investing? To have an investment that takes care of itself, pays you some money each month and appreciates in value, all requiring very little outlay of your time and energy? That's the dream of becoming an anonymous landlord.

You've achieved great things by using your cash to invest in a property or deciding not to sell a property but keep it as an investment instead. These are amazing achievements that only a very small percentage of the population can claim. Most people don't invest.

However, as soon as you take on the management of your properties yourself, you jeopardise all of those potential gains. You're effectively risking any cash flow you generate each month, because one inspection from the local authority has the potential to wipe that out and will more than likely put you into debt. On average, you'll make £3,000–£5,000 a year in net profit on a single property. If you are fined £15,000, you need to have saved at least three years of your profit (if you're making £5,000 a year) just to have the capital to pay the bill. That means three years where you've taken no income from that property.

On top of the fine, you then also have to spend money to do any work required to bring the property up to standard. In addition, your tenant will be able to apply for a rent repayment order, which means they can claim their rent back for the period where the property wasn't up to standard. Plus, you might not be able to rent this property out for a period of time until the work has been done and re-inspected.

I'm not telling you this to scare you, simply to demonstrate that when you manage your properties yourself, you are risking every reason you got into property in the first place, from the financial benefits to the time it takes you to sort everything out and the stress of having to do so. If you don't correctly vet the contractors you use and they aren't correctly insured, accredited and qualified, you could face another fine, not to mention open yourself up to being sued by your tenant. When you compare your vision to this reality, ask yourself whether you really want to manage your property yourself. In fact, most landlords I've spoken to that manage their own properties see it as a bit of a pain in the @rse.

REAP THE REWARDS OF PROPERTY INVESTMENT AND MINIMISE THE RISKS

The very fact that you're reading this book tells me that you don't want to be managing your properties yourself in the way you are now and that you don't want the risk and potential stress associated with doing so. But if this is what you've been doing to date, how can you get out of the management and become the anonymous landlord of your vision? I'll show you how over the coming chapters.

There are three stages I'll talk you through. The first allows you to be a DIY landlord, without doing everything yourself. I'm talking about putting the right processes, practices, protocols, systems, partners and suppliers in place to "do it yourself" but with a strong support network. It's really not that difficult either. The second is to view property as a business and investment, rather than a landlord–tenant relationship. The third stage is how to outsource and automate everything and be a truly anonymous landlord.

At the first stage, you might still be the main point of contact for your tenants, but all you're doing is receiving the information they give you and then allocating it to the right person or people to deal with whatever issue has come up. By the time you reach stage three, you will have empowered the right people to do the right things at the right time to manage your properties autonomously, without sacrificing anything from any of your pots of profit.

I AM THE ANONYMOUS LANDLORD

I have nothing to do with any of my properties, ever. I've never even seen half of my properties – I don't need to and nothing's going to change if I do. I own a letting agency and I have all the systems and protocols in place that, no matter what happens, it all gets taken care of without having to come to me. This would be the same even if I didn't own a lettings management business.

I don't need to authorise anything. I don't need to check anything. I don't need to manage the letting agency. I know that all my tenants are paying a fair market rent. I know that whenever there is anything that needs to be fixed, a qualified and insured tradesperson will take care of it; and I know that I won't be paying to repair damage or issues that are caused by the tenants. If a tenant needs to be evicted, I know it will be taken care of without me. I don't need to get involved in the management or the tenancy at all. I am an anonymous landlord; in fact, I'm more like an anonymous property investor.

I wouldn't class myself as a landlord. To me, the term "landlord" refers to people who are actively landlording. I am not. I don't spend any time on my properties, I don't exchange any energy for more money, I don't give up any time for more money.

What has made the difference? My mindset. I can teach you to be an anonymous landlord like me, where you fill up all of your pots of profit, even if you're a landlord with just one or two properties. Mindset is the key to becoming an anonymous landlord and when you become the anonymous landlord, you are going to succeed more than you could have dreamed of. That's a promise.

I would say that if you only have one or two properties, you are exactly the kind of landlord I'm looking to reach. In my experience, people with just one or two rental properties are most at risk, because they often don't know what they don't know, they undercharge their tenants and that means when there is a large financial outlay or any issue with tenants not paying their rent, they struggle to cover it.

What I'm going to teach you is how to make a profit from property without increasing your risk and without sacrificing your time, energy, mental health and relationships – even if you only have one rental property.

MAKING A MINDSET SHIFT

The key to becoming an anonymous landlord is in shifting your mindset. In many ways it's a subtle change, such as thinking "who can do this for me?", instead of thinking "I can do this myself". As I've mentioned, it's about developing an investor's mindset around your properties, and this is important whether you have one property or 1,000 properties.

A lot of one-to-two property landlords I speak to, who manage everything themselves, don't want to buy any more properties because they feel they don't have enough time to take on more work managing them. I find that quite a shame. With a simple shift in mindset, you can work less, make more money, grow your portfolio and enjoy your money more.

By taking a step back from the management of your properties, you're not only protecting yourself, but also lowering your stress levels. One of the big mistakes many landlords make is that they come to rely on the income they generate from their properties each month. However, this income can fluctuate and it isn't reliable, because there will be higher expenses some months than in others.

THE COST OF RELIANCE ON YOUR PROPERTY INCOME

Adam is reliant on the rental income. When any work is needed at his property he haggles every single invoice, spends hours trying to find other quotes, getting multiple contractors to visit the property and trying to negotiate the lowest possible price. This might save him £50 today but the contractor is unlikely to do the best job, unlikely to want to work for him again and unlikely to prioritise the job. Adam's approach also costs the letting agent a lot more time, frustrates the tenant and annoys the contractors.

Adam also becomes really stressed when a tenant is a day or two late with rent, gets really irritable when there are any deductions from the rent to meet compliance requirements and wants to increase the rent well above market value – all because he is so dependent on the income and can't afford to lose any of it.

This has also led to Adam cutting corners on some more serious work that the tenant has reported. Despite the letting agent's advice, he didn't get the work done properly. The tenant reported it to the council and now Adam has been forced to let the tenant leave with her deposit. He's been ordered to get the whole house done, incurred a fine and been told he must not rent the property out until all work is completed – work he couldn't afford to do.

I actually offered to lend him some money to get this done but he declined. Maybe through pride, maybe something else, but in the end I had to stop my company working with him.

When you're depending on that income, the tendency is to scrutinise every single expense and haggle over everything – in doing so, you become stressed.

That's when you might look at a management fee you're paying and decide that you're better off if you "just do it yourself". It's a slippery slope that sees your profits in every sense diminish, and that takes you further away from the vision you had for becoming a landlord when you started out.

It also prevents you from growing your property portfolio, because when you are doing everything you don't have the time or energy to manage more than a couple of properties yourself, especially if you also have another job.

Always remind yourself why you got into property in the first place: to generate a passive income, to give yourself some financial security and to give you more time and energy to enjoy your life – not to take on another job as a tenancy manager, lettings manager or similar.

As I always say, "What's the point in making profit from property if you've got no time or energy to enjoy it?"

ANONYMOUS LANDLORD ACTION POINT

Make a list of the five pots of profit and give yourself an honest score on how you're performing in each area. Mark yourself out of ten, with ten being the highest and one being the lowest. Which pot (or pots) of profit have you been neglecting?

---

2 THE ANONYMOUS LANDLORD MINDSET

Anna frowns slightly as she pores over the rent statements. Her agent is recommending increasing the rent on two of her properties, both in the same street. It's only an extra £50 a month, but she's worried that, in the current climate, her tenants will look elsewhere. She sighs. Number 2's tenants have been with her for three years, and they've caused very few issues in that time. They're never late with their rent and when they did accidentally break a window, not only did they own up to it and immediately offer to pay, they even checked in with the property manager that they were happy with the contractor they'd chosen. In number 17 is a family who, while newer tenants (just 14 months in), have also been reliable.

Her hand reaches for the phone. "Jean, hi, it's Anna. Thanks for sending over the rent statements. I wanted to talk to you about how we manage this kind of thing moving forward though."

"Of course, what do you have in mind?" Jean asks.

"Well, I'd rather not be dragged into every little decision like this, I'd prefer you to take care of all this for me, so if I share my target profit with you for my properties, can you keep the rent in line with that, without risking any of my tenants leaving?"

"Absolutely," Jean replies. Anna beams at the end of the phone. "Great, let's discuss the rent increase you've proposed here and I'll share my figures, then we can be confident going forward." Anna outlines her current thought process – she's making her target profit from her properties even without the increase

and she'd prefer to keep reliable tenants than potentially lose them when the economy is on its way down.

"I completely understand," Jean says. "Leave it with me from here. I've made detailed notes about everything we've discussed and I'm confident I can keep these properties on track for you."

****

Emily is facing the same dilemma. She owns number 24 on the same street as Anna's properties. Every time she looks at the news, she starts to panic about money all over again, so when her agent called and recommended raising the rent on number 24 by £50, she immediately agreed. She doesn't want to upset her tenants, but she's sure they'll understand. They've been in that house for two years now; she can't imagine they'll want to move.

A week later, Emily's phone rings. She answers it, bright and breezy, "Hello!" "Hi Emily, it's Jean, I wanted to catch up about your tenants in number 24. They have handed in their one-month notice and are going to look for something else. They said they just can't afford the rent increase at the moment. We'll get the property on the market ASAP and I'm sure we'll have someone in within a couple of months."

Emily is shell shocked. All she can think is, "But what if we don't find someone?!" Her mind is racing as she thinks about the mortgage payments, whether she'll need to pay for any updates to the property before she can relet, how much advertising and fees will cost, and the fear that any new tenants will be more difficult to deal with. She's also frantically trying to work out how she can manage without the money from her rental property for a month or two in the worst-case scenario. Emily only manages a muted, "Okay, thanks for letting me know," before hanging up on the call with Jean. She puts her head in her hands – all this for an extra £50.

I'm sure you can see which of the landlords in this story has an investor mindset in this situation, but what exactly is the anonymous landlord mindset and how can you cultivate it? One of the most important components of the anonymous landlord mindset is treating property investment as a business and therefore seeing your tenants as customers. This is a subtle but very important shift in how you approach your properties.

To do this, you need to move your mindset away from thinking of yourself as a landlord (which implies that you handle the management/administration and day-to-day of your property) and instead think of yourself as a *property investor*. Better still – *a business owner*.

The second essential shift for developing the mindset of an anonymous landlord is treating your property like the business it is. I'll come back to what a property business looks like for an anonymous landlord a little later in this chapter.

While business entails everything from managing your income and expenditure to putting systems and processes in place to handle as much as possible, it's changing the way you see your tenants that often makes the biggest difference and that really accelerates your journey to becoming an anonymous landlord.

FOCUSING ON THE HUMAN ELEMENT

Your tenant is your customer. Keep telling yourself that until you truly believe it. When you think about this logically, it really does make perfect sense: you are providing your tenant with a product (their home) and a service (the continued management of that home) and they are paying for it in the same way they would for any other product or service.

Leasing a property is not dissimilar to leasing a car, when you think about it. If you lease a car, you are prepared to pay a monthly fee for a fixed period of time and you can use it as you please. But you don't own that car and, should something go wrong with it, it is the owner (in this case the car leasing company) that will repair the car and foot the bill. Of course, if you clip a pillar in a car park and dent the car, you'll be expected to pay for that repair.

It's the same when you lease a property. You agree to pay rent – sometimes for a fixed period and sometimes on a rolling contract – and if anything goes wrong with the property, it is the owner (aka landlord) who pays for the repairs. Just like with a car, though, if you cause any damage to the home you're in, you are the one who pays for it to be repaired.

Why is seeing your tenant as a customer so important? Because it changes the relationship you build with your tenant. Pretty much every service-based business places a huge focus on looking after its customers. You want to look after them because you want them to continue paying for your services reliably over the long term. You want them to give good feedback and you want to keep hold of the customers who are easy to work with. You want to invest in the services you provide in order to maintain those good customer relationships. You want to do everything possible to retain those good customers.

It's no different when you're talking about tenants. Switching your thinking to see your tenants as customers is part of the bigger picture of becoming an anonymous landlord. The more you treat your tenants like customers, the easier it becomes to keep reliable tenants in your properties and to optimise the rents you charge.

By the way, optimising rent does not mean charging the maximum possible. It means charging the optimum amount to provide you with profitable, reliable, easy, simple, safe property investments. What's the point in charging an extra £50 if you risk having an empty property for three months?

In addition, when you look after your tenants and provide them with a good service, it means they will (usually) treat you the same. If you've ever rented a property yourself and had a bad landlord, you probably didn't care too much about that landlord. That means if your rent was a little late going in, you didn't care if that made them late on their mortgage payments. Why should you care? If they haven't looked after you, why would you want to look after them?

Now think about how you behaved when you rented a property from a good landlord, one who would always fix issues quickly and who took the time to provide you with a great service. I'm willing to bet you never paid your rent late to them and, if for any reason you were going to be late, you probably let them know and explained, rather than just letting the payment deadline go past without a word. How would you rather your tenants treated you?

While it can be easy to think of treating your tenants like customers as taking "effort", this is another switch you need to make to adopt the anonymous landlord mindset. Rather than thinking of this as a cost, whether in your time, energy or money, think of it as an investment that generates a reliable return over the long term. By treating your tenants more like customers and providing them with an excellent level of service, you are creating every landlord's dream – secure, long-term, reliable tenants. This doesn't come at the sacrifice of your profit, by the way.

GREAT CUSTOMER SERVICE = LOYAL, RELIABLE TENANTS

The main areas that fall under customer service as a landlord are providing your tenants with access to fast repairs and maintenance, and making sure that the property they are renting from you is safe, secure, comfortable and hazard-free. When you do this, you significantly increase the likelihood of having long-term tenants.

As in any business, your aim is to develop customer loyalty. There are two main benefits to this, the first being that they will stay with you over the long term and this will bring more stability to your property business. The second is that if you are providing value for money and delivering a great service, when you do need to raise their rent they are much less likely to argue over it.

Retention is an important word to include in your vocabulary as an anonymous landlord. You want to retain your loyal customers, because it costs you money every time a tenant moves out of one of your properties. Empty properties always cost you money as the landlord. Not only do you lose the rent from your existing tenant as soon as they move out, but you then may have a month or even two where you are searching for new tenants. That could easily mean you've lost £1,000 or more in rental income, not to mention any expenses you incur for advertising the property and carrying out viewings.

Whenever you let a property to a new tenant, there is inevitably a cost involved. You also have to pay for the reference checks and vetting of potential tenants, as well as the other compliance you have to carry out. All of this adds up to lost money, time, energy and probably additional stress. You're depleting all of your pots of profit.

THE COST OF PROVIDING POOR CUSTOMER SERVICE

When Frank started out, he was a good landlord. He had a property in a popular area that always rented out quickly. He let it to a couple who moved in and all was well until they reported damp in the flat. Frank treated the problem, which cost around £1,000, and all was well again ... for a while.

The tenants reported more damp – and this time, they moved out. This was the point at which Frank slipped into being a bad landlord. He refused to spend another £1,000. Instead, he just cleaned the walls, painted the area where the damp was visible and relet the property.

Guess what happened over time? Yes, the damp came back! His tenant moved out and Frank repeated the process – clean, paint, relet – against my letting agent's advice. The new tenant moved in, the damp reappeared, that tenant also moved out.

In comes the next tenant and, once again, the damp came back. However, this tenant didn't just move out – they went to the council (uh-oh for Frank!). The council inspected the building and issued a work order to Frank, which cost him a lot more money because the damp had been left untreated and had become worse and worse. That tenant also moved out (surprise, surprise) and Frank wasn't allowed to relet the property until the work was completed. But it gets worse ...

It took another week for the council to reinspect the property and give it the all clear. A new tenant moved in (luckily for Frank, finding tenants was never a problem!). Plain sailing from here? Not quite ...

The property sprung a leak and Frank was out of money! He haggled over quotes, left the leak to get worse and (you guessed it) the tenant moved out. Frank still had to get the leak fixed anyway and then find ANOTHER tenant.

Throughout this process, Frank also spent a lot of time going to the property to "inspect it for himself", even though he'd received formal reports from the inspection that was carried out by qualified experts. He spent lots of time getting quotes, comparing them, haggling and arguing with the lettings team. He was visibly stressed because he relied on this income! Ultimately, the work all got done but Frank lost A LOT more money than he needed to.

In property, the simplest answer is normally the best – but it's not always the cheapest!

Business owners know that it is more expensive to find new customers than to retain existing ones, and it's no different in the world of property. This is why it's so important to view your tenants as customers and to think about the customer experience you're providing.

Take rent rises as an example. Every time you increase your rent, no matter how little or how fair that increase might be, you are prompting your tenant to look elsewhere and find a better deal. Whether they find a better deal or not doesn't matter. The point is you're encouraging them to search which increases the risk of the tenant vacating your property.

By providing excellent customer service and making their experience of renting your property easy, you are creating a unique selling point between you and your tenant that will differentiate you. If you provide an excellent service, your tenant won't want to lose that and will be less likely to jump ship at the first sight of a good deal. Your service will become part of the value of living in this property.

If your tenant can see another property on the same road available for rent for £25 less a month than you're charging, but they know that you fix issues quickly and are a great landlord, it is less likely they'll consider moving. If, on the other hand, you treat your tenants poorly, they may decide it's worth the hassle and upheaval of moving to shave £25 off their monthly rent and to potentially end up with a better landlord.

All this sounds like a lot of effort but it really is not – especially if you adopt the anonymous landlord mindset.

Bad landlords don't think about the retention of tenants – they think about the money. Bad landlords think in the short term rather than the long term. This mentality costs more in both the short term AND the long term. You end up paying anyway, in one way or another (look at what happened to Frank!). You must keep your tenant comfortable and content, otherwise you'll pay for letting a property, loss in rent, the cost of repairs, the cost of problems escalating, fines, work orders, and compensation.

Lots of bad landlords don't see it like this though. They only see the immediate cost of repairs. They cut corners to make a short-term saving but it's false. If you keep doing this, you'll pay in the long run.

THE FINANCIAL ASPECT OF THE ANONYMOUS LANDLORD MINDSET

The aim of any business is to make a profit. As a landlord, you are effectively reselling a product – you are buying a property from a mortgage company for, say, £500 per month and then renting it out for £1,000 to enable you to make that profit, after all your other expenses are factored in.

I can't stress how important it is that your property is profitable, otherwise you won't have enough money to support your property or your tenant. You need to know your income, expenditure, profit and loss across your properties. These are the essential and basic accounting elements that need to be in place. Like any good business, you must make profit in order to continue providing the best service.

From a financial perspective, you also need to factor in regular rent reviews to ensure you're charging a fair market rent. I recommend setting aside one day each month when you have a "money day". I do this myself religiously and I use this time to go over the bank statements for all of my businesses (aka properties) and look at all of my income and all of my expenditures. This means I regularly look for areas where I can optimise my spending on each property.

It also shows me how much profit I'm making and where I might be able to optimise. I love "money day". For me, it's similar to an artist admiring and analysing a piece of art they created. That's cheesy but it's true. It's my chance to reconcile everything I've built and everything I'm building.

For example, can you optimise your mortgage payments if you're coming to the end of a fixed-rate deal? Can you reduce your insurance payments by shopping around for a more competitive quote? Can you find more efficient and cost-effective contractors to maintain your properties? By spending the time carrying out these kinds of financial reviews regularly, you can optimise the profit you generate from your property business.

With my properties, I see this as my role as the anonymous landlord. And guess what? If there are any changes, improvements, savings, or optimisations to be made … I don't do them myself.

PASSIVE INCOME TAKES WORK

Passive income is a term that gets thrown around a lot in relation to property investing. People think they can buy a house, rent it out and the money will just keep coming. As any experienced landlord will tell you, this is not how it works. You have to create passive income, and that takes work.

In fact, even though my property business largely runs itself, I still have a role to play. It's not 100 per cent passive, because I have to give approvals for certain things, I have to deal with my accountant and keep on top of the finances and so on. I prefer to describe my income as automated, rather than passive. I have very little to do with my income sources because I've built them like that, so I'd say it's 90 per cent passive or automated, and ten per cent active.

I have put the systems and people in place that allow me to focus on the areas of my business that need my attention, rather than getting pulled into all the little jobs that can easily be taken care of by someone else. This is why I don't differentiate between property and business. In fact, property IS business. If you treat your property like a business then you'll be able to set it up to work (and grow) without you.

ALWAYS ASK, "WHO CAN DO THIS FOR ME?"

An anonymous landlord can still be a DIY landlord, as long as they have the right infrastructure and structure in place. The difference between a traditional DIY landlord and an anonymous DIY landlord is all in their mindset.

A traditional DIY landlord will think they can save money by doing everything themselves or looking after everything themselves. This is a problem, and I think it comes from the fact that we all live in a property; therefore, it can be easy to think that we know what we're doing and that we might as well sort things out ourselves.

Or, perhaps we are good at DIY; maybe we're tradespeople or something similar. People like this are going to feel like they are able to handle the management of a tenancy. This is not always the case. In fact, I've found that the landlords who work in trades are good at fixing maintenance and repair issues but not so good at the compliance element. Like I said earlier, there are around 170 pieces of legislation in the PRS so, unless you're a letting agent or a property geek, you won't know it all.

An anonymous DIY landlord, on the other hand, will always ask one very important question whenever a tenant comes to them with an issue: Who can do this for me? I'm not only talking in terms of contractors to fix physical issues, but also in terms of the management of the property.

Imagine that a tenant calls you about a leak in their property. Instead of finding a contractor and organising the repair yourself, ask who could manage this for you. Who could call the contractor, arrange the visit and coordinate with the tenant, get and pay the invoice? Asking these questions shifts you towards becoming an anonymous landlord. You could develop a partnership with some contractors and give the tenant their numbers directly OR you could get a letting agent on board to handle everything.

OVERCOMING YOUR FEARS OF STEPPING BACK

The most common objections to this approach stem from your fear. I don't mean that you're trembling at the thought of letting someone else manage everything for you. I mean too many landlords are worried that if they don't manage every step of the process themselves they'll get ripped off, whether that's by a letting agent or a contractor. All too often, landlords focus on the money, rather than considering their other pots of profit.

The antidote to these fears is putting the correct processes and systems in place. For example, a tenant damages the toilet in their property and a plumber goes out to fix it. If the tenant caused the damage, they should be the one who pays for that, not the landlord. If you don't have the right systems in place, the plumber will come to you and you'll have to make that decision, have the discussion with the tenant and so on. It drains your time and energy, even if you don't end up having to pay for the repair. It's the fastest route towards tenant–landlord disputes. You'll want to avoid those.

Let's look at the same scenario when you have a system in place for managing this. A tenant damages the toilet in their property. You have a trusting relationship with your plumbing contractor or a letting agent and there is a system in place whereby, if they can clearly see the damage was caused by the tenant, they bill them directly for the repair. No need for you to get involved and the damage gets repaired. The contractor or letting agent will be able to inform the tenant of this and handle any disputes.

When you're setting up these kinds of systems, you have to think of it in terms of time and money. Do you want to be dragged in every time there's a £60 call-out charge? Probably not. However, if a repair could run into thousands of pounds, you need to be involved in making that decision. You have to put parameters in place so that everyone knows when they should contact you and what they should contact you about.

The instances where you are looking at a bill of thousands of pounds are few and far between, but these are part of that ten per cent of time when you need to take an active – rather than a passive – role in the business.

Another common fear among landlords is of the worst-case scenario. It's easily done, because our brains will naturally take us to worst-case scenarios – if I don't keep control of everything, my contractor will charge me £10,000 for jobs that should only cost £1,000. However, this kind of thinking prevents you from becoming an anonymous landlord. To counter this, you have to develop trust between your contractors and managers, as well as put the systems in place that I've already mentioned.

When you trust your contractors, it's easy to tell them that if a job is urgent, is required to ensure a property is compliant with regulations and it costs less than £200, to just do it without getting your approval. That's step one of the process. Step two is telling your contractors that if a job will cost more than £200, they need to quote you for it.

This gives you the opportunity to source another quote (or even two) if you're suspicious about what they've quoted you. You may decide you want to do this for any larger jobs with all your contractors initially, until you can see their quotes match (or are maybe even cheaper) than others. This all helps build trust that is essential to having these systems in place and running smoothly, allowing you to focus on the aspects of your property business that really need your attention.

I've taken this further with my properties. My rule is, if something needs doing go ahead and get it done. If the invoice is covered by the rent, get it done. If not, come to me. But wait, you're worried that the letting agent or contractor is going to rip you off, right? Let me tell you this: if a company or a contractor is going to rip you off, risk their entire business, risk prosecution, loss of reputation, damage to their business ... they won't do it for £200.

The amount of people who would need to be "in" on the scam is crazy! You'd need the tenant to confirm the job was done, you'd need the contractor to raise an invoice, you'd need a letting agent to be in on it too (if it's managed by an agent). No, the chances are, you're not going to get ripped off. Try this out ... "If it's got to be done, get it done." You'll see the jobs that are carried out on your property, so you can check them if you're uncomfortable. But try it out.

Another common fear among landlords is that if they leave rent collection to someone else, such as a property manager, tenants won't pay their rent. Again, they've gone straight to a worst-case scenario. However, in my experience, it's more effective to have someone impartial whose job is to collect rent (and chase it if it's late), as well as to make sure that the jobs you are paying are being carried out competently and in a reasonable time frame. There are rules around chasing rent and I can safely say that most traditional DIY landlords don't know them.

As a landlord, it can be very easy to become emotionally involved, either with your tenants or properties (or both). You get to know your tenants and become more familiar with them than you would if it was a business and they were its customers. By putting someone impartial in the role of managing your properties, you are removing that emotion. This means better business decisions get made. It also means you don't lose money.

Too many landlords are afraid of losing good tenants, so they find themselves charging well below the market rate because they think "I'd rather keep the tenant happy and I don't want them to leave". I know earlier I said that it's not always the best idea to increase the rent to the maximum it can be but there is a balance. It's still a business and your property investment must still make profit.

The reason a lot of landlords don't keep the rent at fair market value is because they don't want to upset the tenant or lose them. What ends up happening is that the tenant is paying a lot less than they should which effectively means the landlord is giving them money each month.

It's similar with repairs. Some landlords are afraid of confrontations with tenants, so they just pay for any repairs, without pushing back when it is an issue the tenant should be paying to fix. Just to keep the peace! All of this eats into their profit.

The other side of this is that too many landlords rely on the income from their properties, just like Emily in the story at the beginning of this chapter, which means they are constantly looking at ways to cut costs and maintain the same profit. This is a dangerous way of working, because property is an investment not a salary. You might make £500 one month, £400 the next month and then make a £200 loss the following month.

This attachment to the money is what leads them to cut corners, or push back on tenants when they shouldn't. The knock-on effect can be significant; such as the tenant reporting the landlord to their local authority, which results in a fine for non-compliance and a loss of rental income while the problem is fixed.

When you change your mindset to become an anonymous landlord, you are taking the emotion out of the business, and you're putting systems and processes in place that are fair for both you and your tenants. Remember this rule: some months you'll make profit, some months you won't; some months you'll make a lot, some months you'll make a little. Whatever profit you make month by month, your target should be to make profit across the year.

GOOD PRACTICE VS. COMPLIANCE

Compliance with regulations and good practice are two different things. Both are important. According to figures from the Department of Levelling Up, Housing & Communities, 35 per cent of landlords in the UK are compliant with regulations, but don't follow good practice. By contrast, 24 per cent of UK landlords follow good practice, but may be non-compliant with regulations[2].

GOOD PRACTICE: *Looking after your tenants and ensuring they have a comfortable, secure property that is well maintained.*

COMPLIANCE: *Providing the legally required documentation and carrying out checks, such as annual gas safety inspections and electrical installation condition reports.*

That means around a quarter of landlords who think they're doing a good job because they are complying with good practice, are not legally compliant. These people are good landlords, but they're not approaching their business in the right way. Sadly, it's these people who are at risk of being hardest hit. These are also often the landlords who are most worried about remaining compliant and keeping up with all the regulations around property rental. The irony is that becoming an anonymous landlord alleviates this, and many of their other fears.

Then there are the landlords who are compliant but not following good practice – these people aren't good landlords right now, but they have the opportunity to become good landlords. To do so, they need to invest in their property and invest in their relationships with their tenants – treating

---

2 Department for Levelling Up, Housing & Communities, (2022), *A Fairer Private Rented Sector*, June, available at: https://assets.publishing.service.gov.uk/government/uploads/system/uploads/attachment_data/file/1083378/A_fairer_private_rented_sector_web_accessible.pdf

them like customers and shifting from being a landlord to running a property investment business.

In both cases, working to develop the mindset of an anonymous landlord will benefit you.

PROPERTY IS THE EASIEST BUSINESS IN THE WORLD

There are several reasons why property is the easiest business in the world, the first of which is supply and demand. Every single person on the planet wants to live in a property. This means you have an endless customer base and an endless supply of new customers. There are always properties available to buy, and there will always be people who want to rent those properties from you.

Secondly, the business model itself is very simple: you buy a product for X and you sell it for Y. There's nothing more to it than that. Whatever price you pay for the property, you'll be reselling it to your tenants for two or three times that amount. You aren't in a complicated manufacturing business where you have to buy thousands of different components to make one product, as well as set up transport logistics and retail partnerships. It's a very simple model. You're buying a product and reselling it for a monthly fee.

Thirdly, it's an industry that we all know, because most of us live in a home and most of us have a good idea of what a good home should be like. That means, as a landlord, you know what your customers want and how you can make them happy (provided you think of tenants in these terms).

Finally, you have all the add-on industries already in place to support your property business as an anonymous landlord. Contractors, letting agents, mortgage brokers, solicitors and accountants already exist as their own professions; all you have to do is bring them together for your business and make sure that everybody knows what their role in your property business is. Then you can let them get on with their jobs, and you can do yours.

"You are building the easiest business in the world.
Property is business."

ANONYMOUS LANDLORD ACTION POINT

Make a list of all the services you provide to your tenants on a monthly and annual basis. Explore each one in turn and assess whether you are providing good customer service for each. Score yourself out of ten for every service – and be honest! Where could you improve? How can you make a good customer service great?

PART 2:

THE FUNDAMENTAL RULES OF THE ANONYMOUS LANDLORD

Now that we've established you're entering (or are already in) the easiest business in the world, I'm going to explore the fundamental rules of becoming an anonymous landlord. As with much of what you'll find in this book, none of what I'm about to describe is rocket science and, with the right mindset underpinning your property investment, these fundamentals will give you a strong foundation on which to build your property business.

In this second part of the book, I'll take you through what you need to consider when it comes to sourcing a property investment; how to carry out thorough due diligence; what you can do to add value to the properties you buy; and some of the most common options for securing finance to make a property purchase when it's for investment, rather than as your main residence.

Always remember, you are building a business and, as such, you need to think of property investments differently to buying a home you're going to live in. Keep reminding yourself of why you want to become an anonymous landlord – to become financially independent, to give yourself and your family more financial security, and to live life on your terms.

3 SOURCING THE RIGHT PROPERTY

Dave has thought long and hard about what he wants to do with the £50,000 he's inherited. He has been dreaming of having his "money working for him" and, after some deliberation, has decided that buy-to-let property is the way to go.

As he sits down at his computer to start his search for the perfect buy-to-let property, he feels excited. The more he scours the listings on Rightmove, the more encouraged he feels – there are so many properties in his area! Within a week, Dave has over 20 viewings booked through local estate agents and is excited to get started. After a full day of viewings, he heads to his local pub to meet a friend.

"So, how's the property hunt going?" Dom asks. "Viewed about 15 today," Dave says in between sips of his pint. "Reckon I'll offer on seven, maybe eight of them."

"How many properties are you trying to buy? I thought you were starting with one?" Dave gives a knowing smile, "Well I am, but you can't guarantee an offer will be accepted, you've got to hedge your bets." Dom nods. Dave is in full flow now. "I'm being smart about how much I'm offering, doing my research. I'm sure one of them will come through soon."

Dave jumps every time his phone rings, and eagerly picks up when he sees it's one of the estate agents he's been dealing with. However, he's feeling jaded. All the calls have been similar in nature, "Hi Mr Keenan, I'm sorry to tell you that the seller felt the offer was too far below the asking price. Could you go any higher?" Dave stopped trying to argue his offers were fair after the second such call. The estate agents don't care and they certainly don't want to hear him outlining the hours of research he's carried out. "Back to the listings," Dave thinks.

Two weeks later, after many more viewings, Dave's phone rings. "Hi Mr Keenan, I'm just calling about the offer you made on the property on Queens Road, the seller has accepted and would like to proceed." *Dave is speechless. He's trying desperately to remember precisely which property this one is, but his excitement soon gets the better of him.* "That's fantastic news! Let me know what the next steps are and I'll get everything moving my end." *Dave is beaming when he hangs up.*

Four days later, he's sitting at his kitchen counter feeling utterly demoralised. He's just had a call from the estate agent to tell him that the seller of the Queens Road property has changed their mind and accepted a higher offer. He's been gazumped. The estate agent was less than sympathetic when he started to protest, cutting him off with, "I'm sorry, but when you offer below the asking price you always run this risk." *Grudgingly, Dave reaches for his laptop and starts looking at the latest listings.*

One month later, Dave is finally feeling more positive. He's just spoken to his solicitor who confirms contracts have been exchanged, with a completion date set for one week's time. As he walks into the pub that evening, he's all smiles. "I've done it!" *Dave tells Dom as he sits down.* "Exchanged today, completing next week!" "That's great news! Been a bit of a slog to get there, hey?" *Dom says.*

"Tell me about it," *Dave replies.* "But I think this is probably the hardest part, smooth sailing from here on," *raising his glass to toast his first property deal.*

****

Ibrahim opens his laptop and sips his coffee while he waits for his desktop to spring into life. He's got a good feeling about what the day will bring. Sure enough, at the top of his inbox is a reply to the email he sent just three days before – Subject: RE property investing. As Ibrahim reads the email, he starts to smile. Assuming the terms and conditions are fair, he feels this is the one.

Three days later, Ibrahim is once again sitting at his desktop, this time for a meeting with his new sourcing agent. He's got some figures jotted on a pad in front of him and is ready to give them clear instructions about what he's looking for in a property investment. The video call connects and he's greeted by Melanie. After the usual small talk, they get down to business. "So, what kind of property are you hoping to invest in?" Melanie asks. "I'd prefer to get into the family market, so three bedrooms, preferably a garden too. Nothing that needs too much work or modernisation. Did you get the figures I emailed you regarding my budget and the yield I'm looking for on the rental income?" Ibrahim says. "I can get the figures for you now if you don't have them to hand ..."

"No, it's fine. I have them open here on my screen," Melanie replies. "This all looks pretty self explanatory." Half an hour later, Ibrahim is once again sipping coffee. He's confident Melanie knows what he's looking for and now he can get on with the rest of his day.

One week later, Ibrahim's phone rings. Melanie's name flashes on the display. He gives Salma, his wife, an apologetic glance across the table, "I'm sorry, I need to take this. I'll just be five minutes ..." He excuses himself and walks out of the cafe they're sitting in to find somewhere quieter to take the call. "Melanie, hi, do you have some news for me?" He thinks he can almost hear a smile in Melanie's voice. "I certainly do! I've found a lovely three-bed; ticks all your boxes and it's off-market. The owners are looking for a quick sale so they're prepared to take an offer and one that's well within your budget."

"Brilliant! Do I need to view it?" Ibrahim asks. "Not unless you'd especially like to. I've been round it twice and we're having a survey this week to make sure there are no nasty surprises," Melanie explains. "I'll email you all the details now, so you can take a look, but I just wanted to let you know."

Ibrahim thanks her and by the time he's returned to Salma he's smiling. She looks at him with a questioning gaze. "Good news, I take it?" "Sounds like I've found a property to buy. Of course I need to look at the details, but from what Melanie's just told me it sounds like it could be a bargain."

If someone were to hand you £50,000 today, telling you to invest in property, which route would you go down? Would you do all the legwork yourself, like Dave did; or would you find someone to help you, like Ibrahim? If your first thought is to follow Dave's example, you aren't alone. In fact, this is how many property investors approach their search for the right buy-to-let properties.

However, if you engage the services of a sourcing agent, or a property broker, not only do you save yourself a great deal of energy and time, but you also often get better property deals than you can find easily online or via estate agents. I'll talk more about sourcing agents and property brokers, and how you can find one later in this chapter, but let's start by looking at exactly what you need to look for in a property investment.

LOOK FOR PRESS PROPERTIES

PRESS stands for profitable, reliable, easy, simple and safe – and this is precisely the kind of property you should be looking for when you are looking for a rental property to invest in. Each of these five elements will form part of your due diligence (which I'll explore in more detail in Chapter 4).

When you focus on finding a property that hits the PRESS criteria, you take a more objective view of the properties on the market. However, many property investors (especially those who are new to this business) look for properties that "jump out at them". The problem with this approach is that it makes it very easy for you to miss great investment opportunities, just because a property hasn't "jumped out" at you when you've been scrolling through Rightmove, or any other property website. It's likely you're looking for "the perfect deal" or the "ultimate property investment" on the OPEN market. Like everyone else.

Picking the wrong property is also one of the biggest fears of DIY landlords, which often leads to them buying emotionally rather than buying objectively. Most investors, however, will feel that they don't buy emotionally, that they're able to think logically when it comes to buying a property as an investment.

Logically, we all know we need to approach this kind of investment from an objective standpoint, but it can be all too easy to buy for ourselves when looking for investment properties, rather than focusing on staying objective. It takes a lot of experience and skill to be able to remove your fears and feelings from property, relying purely on calculations and due diligence.

The problem is, it's incredibly easy to become emotional when you're buying a property and a lot of the time you don't realise it's happening. I know I've viewed properties and not really liked them, or not felt comfortable in them. Did I walk away from those properties? No, I still bought them because they hit the PRESS criteria.

You have to think about properties like company shares. You might prefer Samsung devices to those made by Apple, but does that mean you won't buy Apple shares when you're investing? Probably not. I often hear property investors saying, "I wouldn't buy a home for a tenant that I wouldn't live in myself." While the sentiment is noble, that's a terrible way to approach property investment. How do you know what your target market of tenants is going to want to live in? Unless you are your own ideal tenant, this won't work. You should treat this like an investment and buy a property for the tenant you want.

Look at it this way: if you live in a five-bedroom detached house in the middle of the countryside and you're viewing two-bedroom terraced houses in an inner city area as an investment, you're not going to like any of them and you're probably not going to want to live in any of them either. If you stick to only buying properties you'd live in, all that happens is you end up buying a property for more money than you should spend and collecting less rent than you've been aiming for.

If you find yourself starting to look at a property through an emotional lens, the first thing you need to do is strip it right back to the numbers. In fact, I would say that the numbers have to come first regardless. Ignore the property in the first instance and just look at the numbers. You're not buying a home, you're buying an investment vehicle. It's that simple.

When you take the emotion out of the decision and approach it from a more ruthless financial perspective, you'll be able to see past the elements of the property that, subjectively, you might not like. I'm not saying you have to ignore those subjective elements forever, but in the first instance you want to make sure all of your objective boxes are ticked. I'm talking about the purchase price, rent value, yield, supply and demand, and due diligence.

Once you know all your objective boxes are ticked, you can start looking at what you might change on a subjective level. Remember that if property is your business, then each rental property you buy is your product, the tenant is your customer and landlording is your service. You want a customer to buy your product. In the case of property, you might be buying it with a mortgage of £500 per month and renting it to a tenant for £1,000 a month, which also pays for the service you're providing. That's basic business. The cost of your product should be less than the price your customers pay.

By providing this service, you are aiming to keep your customers loyal. To do this, you need to see the value in your product (property) and service (landlording) because when you do these two things well, tenants will be more inclined to keep renting from you, reliably.

One of the ways in which to ensure you're delivering a high level of service and a good quality product is to enhance the tenant's subjective elements of the property. So, the subjective aspects of a property, such as the quality of the flooring or the decor, can be used to enhance your objective goals as a property investor.

This comes back to what I talked about in Part 1 in terms of getting into the mindset of an anonymous landlord. A loyal, valuable customer in any business will appreciate the product and service that business provides. As a landlord, your job is to optimise, enhance and improve your investment vehicle (the property) to create that loyalty and help your tenants see the value in your services as a landlord.

A fundamental difference between a good landlord and a bad landlord is this willingness to enhance and optimise each property. A good landlord will see the value in constantly improving their investment vehicle, because they know their tenants will value these improvements and therefore that they're more likely to remain loyal and less inclined to look elsewhere. A bad landlord, however, won't make these improvements and this means their tenants will not only be inclined to pay less, but that they're also more likely to be looking for somewhere else to live and to leave at the first opportunity.

Everyone has heard stories of bad landlords. These are normally landlords who don't look after the property, don't keep it in a good state and don't look after the tenants. These are the landlords who don't manage their investment properly. There is a link between the best property investors and the best businesses in the world: all of them look after their products. All of them continuously improve their products. All of them look after their customers. All of them work on providing a good service. Property is business. If you maintain a good product, you'll maintain good customers.

HOW TO MAKE SURE YOU TICK YOUR OBJECTIVE BOXES WHEN SEARCHING FOR AN INVESTMENT PROPERTY

The first step is to make sure you know what your objective boxes are when you're searching for an investment property. An experienced property investor will have these in mind when they're looking at property listings (if they don't have a sourcing agent or property broker doing this for them). The key is to focus on these objective criteria and to discount anything subjective that could cloud your opinion of a particular property. Sounds simple, right?

This is easier said than done, especially when you don't have a great deal of experience in property investing. It can be easy to discount properties in a certain area because you don't like it, or to rule out properties you don't like the look of when you are new to this. However, being able to focus on facts and figures rather than subjective criteria is fundamental if you are to make successful property investments.

The following are the objective boxes you need to tick when looking for a property investment:

- Price
- Number of bedrooms/size of property
- General location
- Fair market value
- Rent value
- Yield
- Additional spend required

Let's imagine you're looking for a family home to rent out and you have an upper budget of £220,000. We're going to mention yield here, and it's important to know that there are three different types of yield:

- **GROSS YIELD** – a method of uniforming a wide range of properties but this is NOT your return on investment.

- **CASH YIELD** – calculates the profit you generate from the actual cash you've invested. It's the simplest kind of yield calculation.

- **TRUE YIELD** – cash yield PLUS growth in value. This is the full return on investment.

We'll go through yield calculations another time.

You see a property on the market for £200,000 ✔

It has three bedrooms ✔

It's in the right general location ✔

Based on your research, it has a fair market value ✔

It rents for £1,000 per month ✔

Your yield will be ten per cent ✔ (cash invested versus profit)

From the photos, you can see it needs about £2,000 to be spent on it ✔

Once you know all of those boxes have been ticked, you can consider some of the more subjective elements, such as whether you want to replace the living room carpet or repaint the exterior of the property. Whether you are planning to search for properties yourself or you intend to use a sourcing agent, you will need to know what each of those objective criteria is for the property business you want to build.

REMEMBER WHO THE ESTATE AGENT IS WORKING FOR

In my experience, many untrained property buyers will either trust that the estate agent they're dealing with is acting for them, or expect that the agent will be acting in their best interests. A lot of buyers make complaints about estate agents for acting in the seller's best interests! If you're going to be the best property investor you can be, always remember that the estate agent is acting on behalf of the seller and their sole job is to sell that property for as much money as possible. Buyers do not instruct or pay estate agents to act for them. The agent's customer is the seller.

A good estate agent will have their own checklist that they're looking for in a buyer, which will likely include:

- Whether a buyer can proceed with the purchase

- Whether a buyer can complete quickly (because the estate agent doesn't get paid until the sale goes through)

- Whether a buyer is reliable and will therefore uphold the estate agent's reputation with their customer

An estate agent will do what's required in order to get you to buy a property, because it's in their interests to do so. That's not a dig at estate agents, they're just doing their job. Good estate agents go about their business in an honest and methodical way. However, many untrained property investors will forget who the estate agent is working for, they will forget their objective checklist and processes, and they'll jump into an investment that isn't right for them. You have to assume that the estate agent is not working for you, is not acting in your interests and, as such, you must trust your own instinct, due diligence and calculations.

A TRUE BUT CAUTIONARY TALE

One of my clients came to me and told me he wanted to buy an investment property. He outlined what he was looking for and stressed he wanted a property with a good yield. I started having a look at what was available. A few days later, he called me. "Tom, I've agreed to purchase a three-bedroom flat. The block's a bit shitty, but it's on for £170,000 and the estate agent told me it currently rents at £1,350 per month!"

However, while what the estate agent had told my client was true, what they failed to mention was that the flat was currently rented to three students who were each paying £450 per month for a single room each. It wasn't licensed as an HMO (house in multiple occupation), and the students were due to move out shortly after the sale completed. As it happened, the estate agent claimed afterwards that the seller told them this property had the correct licence in order to be used as an HMO. Do I believe that? Not sure.

At the time, my client didn't know any of this. All he knew was that he could buy it for £170,000 and rent it for £1,350 per month, or so he thought. What a deal! He bought the flat, the students moved out and then he was stuck with a three-bedroom flat in a crappy block that needed a full refurbishment. In addition, he couldn't get an HMO licence for it, so he has to rent it as a standard residential letting for £800 per month.

It gets worse ... The block management company wrote to him a while later to inform him that there were major renovation works planned for the building and his share would be £10,000. While this work was not formally in place during his purchase, it's another poke in the eye for my client. It wouldn't have been so bad if the rent had actually been £1,350 because there would have been plenty of profit to cover this work.

He got burned because he thought the estate agent was helping him out by highlighting this great deal: he was blinded by the deal and completely forgot the due diligence. In the end, he tried to sell the flat but couldn't get any offers that were anywhere near what he paid for it. It was an expensive lesson to learn.

WORKING WITH A SOURCING AGENT OR PROPERTY BROKER

As I mentioned at the start of this chapter, a sourcing agent or property broker will find properties for you that tick all of your objective boxes and, to demonstrate that the properties they're bringing you are suitable, they will usually do these calculations and present them to you alongside the property's details. If you engage a sourcing agent or property broker, ask them to provide comparison evidence for each investment property they recommend to make sure you're on the same page.

You normally have to pay a sourcing agent or property broker for their services, but this is typically because you're buying a property below market value and you wouldn't have ever known about it without the sourcing agent or property broker. Plus, the time and energy it can save you is significant. That's not to mention the fact that sourcing agents and property brokers will often be able to find properties that aren't for sale on the open market. I pay a sourcing fee all the time, it's just part of the investment.

You might think a sourcing agent or property broker sounds great, but your next question is likely to be, "How on earth do I find one?" In all honesty, sourcing agents and property brokers are desperate to find you, but you're not going to be walking around wearing a T-shirt that says, "I'm a property investor, come and speak to me". That means you have to make sure sourcing agents and property brokers know who you are.

Among the simplest ways to start looking for a sourcing agent or property broker are to post in relevant Facebook or other social media groups, and to network with other property investors and ask them if they know of any sourcing agents or property brokers. Word will spread quickly and you'll find that agents and brokers often come to you.

In my experience, anonymous landlords use sourcing agents or property brokers because it saves them a great deal of time, energy and money because they are making good property investments rather than choosing poorly and having to sell properties to reinvest. I would always prefer to pay a fee for a much better property investment with a much higher yield than do all the legwork myself and end up with a regular property and a regular yield.

A sourcing agent or property broker can also help you with the legwork when it comes to your due diligence. You can ask them to compile a report containing supply and demand statistics, details about similar properties within a quarter of a mile of yours that have been sold in the last year, information about other properties on the market, and the condition of rental properties.

By taking this approach, you're behaving like a CEO and treating property like a business. You can then look over all of this information, decide whether you agree with it or whether you'd like to investigate further and then make a decision about whether a property is the right investment for you.

As with any relationship, you need to develop trust with your sourcing agent or property broker and that can take time. You may look closely at the first three or four properties a sourcing agent or property broker brings you, but once you can see they have a good track record, you might decide to trust their judgement and save yourself the time.

For example, I work with a sourcing agent whom I trust implicitly. When we first started to work together, I'd look over all the evidence for each property before agreeing to a purchase. Now, however, all it takes is a quick phone call where he tells me a bit about the property, the valuation and the comparison evidence and I'll say yes or no then and there.

Remember that property is a business and you are the CEO. All you're doing is getting other people to gather the information and evidence you need to make a decision. Remember the dream that encouraged you into property investment in the first place: to become an anonymous landlord. You might still choose to view the properties you're buying, I do sometimes because I quite enjoy it, but I don't *have* to.

By the way, I'm definitely NOT telling you not to keep doing your due diligence. My point here is for you to get other people to do it for you.

"When you become an anonymous landlord,
you're giving yourself the freedom to choose."

ANONYMOUS LANDLORD ACTION POINT

Go into whichever property investment groups you're part of on social media platforms and write a post asking for recommendations for sourcing agents and property brokers. You'll be surprised by the response you get!

---

4 DUE DILIGENCE

Now that the contracts have been exchanged, Dave finally feels confident that he can plan the refurbishment and get everything ready for the property to go on the market and rented out as soon as possible. Just two days to completion!

He's going over his figures again, but he's feeling good. The previous owner accepted an offer of £140,000 because they wanted a quick sale and some of the properties on that street have sold this year for around £180,000 – not that he's planning to offload it any time soon. He picks up his phone and dials the number of his letting agent.

"Hi Suri, it's Dave Keenan, you asked me to call you back to discuss the rental of 27 Clarence Road?" After the usual back and forth, they get down to the purpose of the call. "I was looking to put it up for rent at the £1,100 per month mark," Dave says.

Suri pauses. "That might be a bit high for that property, I'd recommend going in at the £900–£950 mark," she says.

"Why?" Dave asks, confused. "I've seen a couple of other houses on that street on the rental market for £1,100, one's even on for £1,200, and it's only a few doors down!"

"I know that there's a bit of a range on that street," Suri replies, "but the properties that rent at those levels have loft conversions, which means they've got an extra bedroom. It makes quite a difference." "Ahh, I see," Dave says, once again starting to feel deflated.

As their conversation continues, Dave crosses out the £1,100 he has written on his budget and replaces it with £950. Suri's voice brings him back to the discussion, "Mr Keenan? When did you say you expect it to be ready to rent, and when would we be able to get photos of the property?"

"I'm aiming to have the refurb completed within three weeks, so it would be great to have some tenants lined up for ..." Dave checks his calendar, "mid-September? That's five weeks away, so it will give me a bit of breathing space."

"Okay, thank you. We'll put together a listing with the existing pictures, stating that it's undergoing a refurbishment and will send that for your approval before we start marketing it," she says. "Great, thank you," Dave replies.

As he hangs up on the call, he returns to the pages of notes spread across his kitchen table. The big £950 stands out at him, and he sighs, "Time to recalculate. That will mean I have a bit less to spend on the refurb," Dave thinks to himself.

****

Ibrahim is staring intently at his computer screen. He's got a pad of paper and a calculator to one side, and it's covered in figures and workings. He squints slightly as he makes notes on the figures he's scrolling through. Melanie, true to her word, has done her due diligence. She's sent him a spreadsheet detailing the sale prices of similar properties to his over the last three years, as well as the rental values of other properties on his street.

He was very clear about wanting at least a ten per cent yield on the rental and, looking at the other similar properties that let for around £950 per month, he's confident he can get it. Maybe a bit more after the refurb. Salma gives his study door a cursory tap as she pushes it open. "Tea?" She asks. Ibrahim smiles, *"Please, yes."* She returns with a cup in each hand, *"How's it all looking?"* She asks.

"We should easily be able to let it for £950 a month, but I think if we replace the kitchen and bathroom, as well as doing a full redecoration and tidy up of the garden, we could get £1,000," he explains. *"Can we afford that level of refurbishment?"* *"That, my dear, is just what I'm about to work out,"* Ibrahim says with a grin. He shows Salma his estimates for each element of the refurb, *"And I'm allowing ten per cent over that figure, just in case."* *"That seems workable?"* She responds.

Ibrahim nods, *"It does. I just want to go over my figures one more time though, make sure there's nothing I'm missing. I'm also going to take a look at the other houses on the street that rent for the £1,000 mark to see if there's anything we can do to stand out."* Salma smiles, *"I will leave you to it!"*

Due diligence is not just about the property you're looking at; it's about making the shift to being a business and investor, rather than just seeing yourself as a landlord. Investing in property is like investing in any other asset class, and you need to carry out due diligence on any major investment.

There are several elements you need to consider as part of your due diligence before you invest in a specific property. They are:

- Value
- Supply and demand
- Trends
- Cash yield
- True yield
- Cash employed
- Worst-case calculations

CALCULATING A PROPERTY'S VALUE

There are three values you need to look at when you're assessing a property as an investment as part of your due diligence: the sale value, the mortgage value and the rent value. For each of these, you need to work out the top (optimistic), middle (realistic) and bottom (worst case) values. For the sale and rent values, you're essentially making educated guesses.

SALE VALUE: you can work this out based on what similar properties in the same area have recently sold for. I would recommend going ten per cent either side of your middle value to calculate your top and bottom values. Sale values are what estate agents provide and they arrive at their figures by considering supply and demand, as well as the local property market. Often their valuations are on the optimistic side.

TIP: don't calculate your sale value using properties that are not sold. Advertising price is NOT sale price. A property is only worth the price someone is prepared and able to pay for it. Unsold properties are just that.

RENT VALUE: as with the sale value, you can base this estimate on what other similar properties are being rented for in the same area. Again, go ten per cent either side to get your upper and lower values.

ANOTHER TIP: only use let-agreed prices, don't use prices of properties that have not been let. You can advertise a property for as much as you like, but if it's not let then it's irrelevant.

MORTGAGE VALUE: this is a purely evidence-based calculation by your lender. Financial institutions calculate mortgage value in a couple of ways. One is to look at sold properties relative to yours and, if there are no precise comparisons, they look at the square meterage of the property. So, if two similar properties on the same road have recently sold for £200,000, the mortgage value is likely to be £200,000. It's important to remember that the chartered surveyors who usually carry out these valuations don't consider supply and demand as evidence, or the other properties on the market, they base their calculations on objective evidence.

Knowing these values helps you in several ways. Firstly, knowing the sale value ensures you have an exit strategy and can give you confidence that, if you go ahead with the purchase but it doesn't work out, you can get your money back by selling the property. Secondly, knowing the rent value allows you to calculate the income – and more importantly profit – you can get from the property. It's vital to make profit.

Thirdly, the mortgage value will determine the finance you can get for the purchase. It's important to work this value out early on, so that you don't get halfway through the process only for your mortgage lender to undervalue the property compared to what you were expecting based on the sale value. Finally, by knowing all these values you can make sure you're paying the right price for the property and that this is a good investment.

CALCULATING SUPPLY AND DEMAND

It's very simple to calculate supply and demand – you just need to look at the number of properties on the market versus the number of properties that are sold and let. Rightmove has made this process even easier, because you can create a list of all properties of a certain type or size (say three-bed houses) in a given area. You can also include sold properties in this list by adding this as a filter. So, if there were ten properties on the market and ten that had been sold, supply and demand would be well-balanced and healthy.

If a low number of properties have been sold compared to the number of properties on the market (for example 20 properties on the market and just five that have sold), that is a sign of low demand. Conversely, a high number of sold properties is a sign of strong demand (I'm sure you get the picture). As an investor, you're looking for properties that have good to strong demand. The more demand, the better your investment.

You'll often find that the property sale ratios are very similar to rental ratios, purely because this is all about where people want to live rather than whether they want to rent or buy. Of course, where people want to live will depend on various factors. Some of the most common are schools, employment and infrastructure. While the sales and rental markets generally track one another, an exception is areas where property is expensive. In these locations there tends to be a lower rental market.

Why is all of this important as an anonymous landlord? Because you want to make sure you have an exit from your investments. If you buy a property that has a very low sale demand, it will be harder for you to sell it and exit that investment if you ever need to. Looking at supply and demand allows you to very quickly see how easy or difficult it will be to sell a property or to rent it out.

TOP TIP

If you're asking someone else to source properties and provide you with information, make sure you give them clear instructions. I give sourcing agents and property brokers a checklist to follow so they know exactly what a property investment looks like for me. What you need to know to calculate supply and demand is the number of properties on the market that are similar to the one you're planning to buy, how many of those properties have sold, and what property sales have been completed historically. The data needs to be for properties that are as comparable as possible to your potential investment.

Knowing supply and demand for your properties helps you identify their risk factors as well as your positioning. For example, if you want to buy a three-bedroom house and can see that other similar rental properties are on the market for between £900 and £1,100 per month, you can compare the properties renting for £900 to those renting for £1,100 and identify the difference.

In doing so, you can get a good idea of where to position *your* property. Let's say you're planning to refurbish your property to a good standard. You can see that the properties renting for £1,100 look stunning throughout and are fitted with expensive kitchens and bathrooms. You're planning to fit a standard kitchen and bathroom, which will be nicer than the properties at the cheaper end of the market, but not as fancy as those at the top end. Therefore, you'd position your rent around £1,000 per month.

Personally, I never try to have the most expensive properties in the area because this means fewer people will be attracted to your property. I also make sure I've never got the cheapest either. If there are ten properties on the market for between £900 and £1,100, people will look at the ones in the £900–£1,000 range first, because they want to try to rent the same property for a lower price.

By sitting in the middle to upper end of that range, your property will get noticed by more potential tenants and will stand out as being of a higher quality than the cheapest options. The mid-market is the biggest – the people who don't want cheap crap but also can't afford the most expensive. That's the biggest market: the best of both.

Understanding supply and demand will also give you an insight into how quickly your property will be rented out once it goes on the market. Generally speaking, the highest priced properties on the market are the slowest to rent out, which is another argument for positioning your property in the mid-range.

LOOKING FOR TRENDS TO HELP BOOST YOUR PROPERTY'S APPEAL

The supply and demand information also presents an opportunity to identify trends within the property market. This is something that very few property investors and landlords do, but it can make a big difference to how easily you can rent your property and how much you can ask for it.

Let's imagine that there are 20 comparable properties on the market in your area and ten of these are sold. What is different about the ten that have sold? Are there any similarities between them? Are they decorated in similar colour schemes or carpet colours? Do they all have a similar style of kitchen that the ten unsold properties are missing? You can also do it the other way around. What are the trends and similarities of properties that have not sold.

What you're looking for is any clue about what made those ten properties more popular than the ten that have yet to sell. You can carry out the same exercise in the rental market by looking at the properties that have rented versus those that haven't. The more you do this kind of comparison, the more you'll notice the subtle differences that could be down to whether a property has a lawn or a patio, whether it's double glazed or not and even the quality of the front door.

This information can also be incredibly useful if you're planning to refurbish the property and can help you make decisions about the features you'll include or decor you'll choose. This comes back to what I talked about earlier in terms of seeing your property as a product and your tenants as customers. It's important to be aware of market trends, and follow those where it's practical to do so.

As I'm writing this, if you were to search for rental properties on Rightmove you'd see lots of refurbished houses with white walls and grey carpets, because that's what loads of investors and landlords think everybody wants. Of course, that's not always the case. In fact, many people prefer to have a bit of colour.

Rather than white walls and a dark grey carpet, I would recommend having light grey walls with a feature wall in a colour like navy or teal (a fashionable option at the time of writing), and this is the kind of trend you can identify by carrying out this basic comparison exercise. Again, check the trends and follow what works. Copy and paste your way to success!

A WORTHWHILE INVESTMENT ...

Elaine bought a property and refurbished it with white walls and grey carpets – classic refurb! She marketed it to let at the higher end of rental values in the area because it was newly refurbished, but it didn't let as quickly as she'd hoped. There were lots of viewings but it just didn't appeal to the applicants. Elaine went back to the drawing board.

Looking at the market, she saw that the standard properties in this area (a three-bed house in Portsmouth) were renting at the time for £900. The most expensive property available to market was £1,000, which had better decor and a really nice garden. She spent £500 on wallpaper and made a feature wall in each room; as well as installing a new front door, better lighting, and creating a more attractive and functional garden. It rented for £1,000.

Elaine spent around £2,000 more on the refurb, and ended up getting an extra £1,200 per year. That means she got her additional investment back in 20 months. PLUS, she increased the value of the property.

Simple things like this can either be seen as a cost or an investment. Elaine invested a little bit more money which secured her a better return on investment, increased the asset's value and resulted in a more appealing product (property). Plus, tenants are more likely to stay longer term in a nicer property.

The advice here is to create a product which is targeted to your ideal customer. If you want the top-end customers, you must create a top-end product. If you want low-end customers, create a low-end product. Whatever you do, think of it as an investor who is investing in their property business.

This is just basic business sense. You need your product (property) to compete with the others that are popular in the market. That means if you can see that the people you want to rent your property are leaning towards those with light grey walls and a stronger colour feature wall, it's common sense to decorate your property in a similar fashion to appeal directly to them. You're not going to reinvent the wheel and you don't need to. There are so many successful property investors and all their successful products are right there for you to copy.

Your job, as the owner of this property business, is to make sure your products are seen first and that people want to view and try out your product. The simple fact is that the more people that are attracted to your product, the faster it's going to sell, or in this case, rent.

CALCULATING THE CASH YIELD FOR A PROPERTY

Your cash yield is simply the calculation of the amount of actual cash you are putting into your property investment and the amount of actual cash you are getting out (profit). This is very different to gross yield, which is what many people use incorrectly. Gross yield is more like a universal marker than a yield and therefore not that helpful for a property investor to calculate the actual return on investment

To calculate your cash yield, you start by working out how much cash you need to put into finishing the project. Note that I've said finishing and not "buying". What you need to calculate is how much cash you will have to spend before you start generating any cash back. Once you have this figure, you then need to work out how much physical profit you will be left with once you are generating an income.

Begin with your cash investment. Add up your deposit, stamp duty, legal costs, broker fees, lender fees, survey fees and any other costs associated with actually buying the property. Then add in the rest of your cash investment, which will include refurbishments, mortgage payments, letting costs, insurances, licences and refinancing costs. In a nutshell, this is all of the physical cash that comes out of your pocket. You get the idea. This cash investment is the entire amount of physical cash you are investing in this project, all the way up until the point you start getting physical cash back.

Let's say that you've worked out that you will spend £60,000 to get the property rented. Once the tenants are in, you know you're going to receive £1,000 a month in rent, less the mortgage payment, insurance payments and management fee. In this example, let's say that leaves you with a profit of £500 per month, or £6,000 per year. That £6,000 is ten per cent of your initial cash investment and that is your cash yield. *Ten per cent.* It means your cash is generating ten per cent of itself every year. Of course, you keep your cash invested too. Win-win.

It's really important to work out your cash yield so that you can see quickly (and before you have gone ahead with the purchase) whether it will deliver a good enough return. I would say that you want to aim for a minimum cash yield of ten per cent; any less than that and you could probably do better.

For my property investment calculations (and for my clients), I created a brilliant Excel spreadsheet which works it all out for me. I enter the main pieces of information and the document calculates ALL my yields, forecasts and costs. You should do the same.

CALCULATING YOUR CASH EMPLOYED

Cash employed simply means the amount of cash you have to "employ" to complete the project. So, if we take the example from our cash yield calculation, the cash employed would be £60,000. In a nutshell, it's an active figure that reflects the amount you will need to buy, refurbish and rent out a property.

It's important to distinguish cash employed from cash working, however. Cash working is what is left in the investment after the project is completed. This cash is now "working" for you (as in the case of property, once it's rented out). For example, you might have £60,000 of cash employed, but once you've finished the project and rented it, you refinance the property leaving just £20,000 in that property. This means your cash working is £20,000.

If you look at the example I shared about calculating your cash yield, if you refinanced after completing the project and only left £20,000 in the property, you need to use this figure (rather than the £60,000) to calculate your cash yield.

Therefore, in this rough example you "employ" £60,000 of your cash to complete the project. After you complete the project, you leave £20,000 of your cash "working" for you.

CALCULATING YOUR TRUE YIELD

Your true yield takes the figures from your cash yield and adds to them. This is a concept that I came up with, so it's not a calculation that many property investors will do, but I believe it's important because it factors in the growth in value of your asset over time.

Let's stick with our previous example, where we have a ten per cent cash yield on a property bringing in £6,000 in profit per year. To calculate your true yield, you take this figure and add the amount your property increases in value each year. To keep things simple, let's say this particular property increases in value by £6,000, which is very realistic. That means you're making £12,000 per year, or a true yield of 20 per cent.

Of course, to get that additional £6,000 in hard cash, you'd need to sell the property, but that additional growth in value of £6,000 is still yours even if you hold onto your property for 20 years – it's all your money. Think of it like bank accounts. You have a current account, a savings account and an equity account. The only difference between each of your accounts is in how long it takes to withdraw that cash. So, don't worry about leaving some cash in your equity account. In many cases, it's more profitable than leaving it in your current account.

The beauty of true yield is that it compounds. This means that if property prices consistently go up by three per cent a year, the amount of money you make grows more quickly. So, if you bought a property for £200,000 and it rose in value by three per cent, at the end of year one you'd have a property worth £206,000. Assuming it continues to increase by three per cent a year, by the end of year two it would be worth £212,180, and at the end of year three it would be worth £218,545 and so on. The point is, it will keep rising faster and faster.

It can be difficult to forecast the future growth value of a property, but using historical price growth you can get a fair idea of where a property's value is likely to go in the coming years. Most people invest in property for the long term. If you're planning to hold onto a property for 20 years, you can look back at how the price has increased over the last 20 years to get an indication of how much it's likely to increase in the coming 20 years.

In my experience, one of the biggest fears property investors have is of their property's value decreasing. Whenever the house price index shows property prices are falling, some investors panic. But my question to any of my clients who are worried is always, "Are you planning to sell your property this year?" Invariably the answer is "No", in which case I tell them not to worry. Firstly, because there have been very few occasions when property prices have fallen dramatically; and secondly, because even when they have, they haven't remained low for 20 years.

As long as your property is rented out, you are in a good position, even if the objective value of your property falls for a few months or years. In fact, if your business is renting properties, falling property prices can actually be a positive. Usually, if property prices fall it means interest rates have risen, which in turn means fewer people will be able to get a mortgage and therefore more people will need to rent. People always need properties.

The point I'm making is that you need to have a long-term investor mind-set. This is also part of the anonymous landlord mindset I talked about in Chapter 2.

ALWAYS PLAN FOR THE WORST

It's important to always plan for the worst-case scenario, especially when it comes to refurbishing properties. My advice is to always add ten per cent of the anticipated cost as a contingency. So, if I'm planning to spend £10,000 on refurbishing a property, I'll allow £11,000 for that project, because you never know what might happen. It could be something simple like some of the plaster coming off when you peel wallpaper off, or the kitchen you wanted increasing in price from £5,000 to £6,000.

You also have to consider the worst case when it comes to finding tenants, such as by thinking about what you'll do if it takes you three months to rent the property once it's ready, or what you'll do if you get a tenant in and then have to evict them later in the year because they're not paying rent. The reality is that it can take up to eight months to evict a tenant for non-payment of rent – which sounds scary – but actually, this just means you can calculate how much that will cost upfront and plan for that eventuality.

So, if it takes eight months to evict a tenant, you might need to cover the mortgage payments and insurance payments for eight months. Whenever I think about the worst-case scenario, I put a number on it. What is the actual cost of this worst case scenario? £3,000? £2,000? A number is not as scary as the fear of the worst case.

THE PRESS TEST

In the last chapter I talked about looking for PRESS properties. Once you've completed your due diligence, it's a good idea to put any property investment you're considering through the PRESS test. As a reminder, PRESS stands for profitable, reliable, easy, simple, safe. Let's look at what your due diligence will show you for each of these areas:

- **PROFITABLE:** your yield and cash flow calculations will show you whether the property is going to be profitable. You MUST make profit.

- **RELIABLE:** this is about how reliable your income will be, the type of tenant you'll attract, and the demand for the property. It's vital to make sure you have the most reliable income from this property.

- **EASY:** this encompasses supply and demand, so the question is: will it be easy to rent out? But also, will it be easy to exit from the investment if you need to? Easy in, easy out.

- **SIMPLE:** this speaks to the complexity of the investment. Simple property investments are often the best. There's a reason the most successful property investors don't chase high yields, and instead chase simple property investments.

- **SAFE:** is it a safe investment? That means, is it a property that will have high demand, in an area where the rental market is strong? For example, a three-bedroom house is usually a safer investment than an HMO or an unusual property, because it has the largest target market. If that house is also in an area with a strong rental market and doesn't have any complications (like those I just shared), you can consider it a safe investment.

DEVELOPING THE RIGHT MENTALITY FOR DUE DILIGENCE

The process of due diligence is designed to ensure you are making a safe investment that will deliver a reliable profit. Not every property investment you look at will be straightforward, but that doesn't necessarily mean you should walk away from them. Due diligence isn't about looking for reasons *not* to buy a property, but about working out *how you can* buy a property.

You need to make sure you're not approaching due diligence with the mentality of looking for bad things in a property, because if that's what you're focusing on then that's what you'll find. The due diligence process is there to help you figure out how you can buy a property investment and how much you should buy it for. Remember, every property has a price. Your job is to calculate the price of the property as an investment.

I'll give you an example. Let's say I view a property that's on the market for £200,000 and the estate agent has told me they think it needs about

£10,000 of work. After viewing the property, I estimate that it needs closer to £30,000 of work on it. A lot of people would decide to walk away at that point, but I take a different approach – I ask *how* I can still buy this property.

It needs £20,000 more work than I thought, but it's not just as simple as offering £20,000 less, because my risk goes up with a bigger refurbishment project. In that case, I might offer £25,000 or £30,000 less and, of course, that offer might get rejected, but what I've done is used the information I've gathered through my due diligence to make an offer that works for my business in terms of yields and cash flow. When you approach the due diligence process with this mentality, you will see properties for what they are – investment assets – and you will likely make smarter business decisions.

It's also VITAL to share your calculations openly and honestly with the estate agents and the sellers. It's hard to argue logically against calculations. Be honest about your profit margin. You're entitled to make a profit. After all, you're investing your own cash.

I always say, "A property is just a pile of bricks,"
because that removes any emotion from that property.
If I don't win a property deal, "it's just a pile of bricks".
If I do win a property deal, "it's just a pile of bricks".

ANONYMOUS LANDLORD ACTION POINT

Calculate the cash yield for your next investment property, or your most recent property investment if you've purchased one in the last year. Are there any figures you don't have easily to hand? If so, make a note of what those are. Create your own spreadsheet to save time on the due diligence for your next investment, and to ensure you include all the data you need in your property investment calculations.

5 ADDING VALUE TO PROPERTY INVESTMENTS

The sunlight is beginning to fade as Dave arrives at number 27 Clarence Road. As he opens the door and steps inside, he sighs. The refurb is taking longer than he'd hoped – although the new bathroom is in and the upstairs rooms are pretty much ready, he still has all of the downstairs rooms to paint.

He goes straight to the kitchen and puts the kettle on. Just as it's boiling, there's a knock at the door. He turns and heads back down the hall. "Dom, mate, thanks so much for popping round and helping out this evening." "Not to worry, I've always been a dab hand with a paintbrush," Dom replies with a smile. "Where are we starting?"

"Living room tonight, new carpet is going in tomorrow. Do you want a coffee? Kettle's just boiled ..." "An extra dose of caffeine won't hurt!" Dom answers. Coffees in hand, they get to work masking around the skirting boards and ceilings. "Which paint are we using?" Dom asks.

"Any of those cans are fine – I'm keeping it simple: magnolia on all the walls!" Dave says. Dom nods, testing the weight of the cans to find the one that's already open. Between the two of them, it doesn't take long to paint the living room. "Want to make a start on the hallway too?" Dom asks. "Sounds good, mate!" Dave says, relieved that they've made such good progress. "At this rate it might just be ready in time ..." he thinks.

Three days later, he's back at number 27 feeling much more optimistic. The new carpets are in; just a few finishing touches, and the gas safety inspection tomorrow, and he should be good to go. His phone buzzes as he opens the door and he starts reading the text message as he steps inside. Dave stumbles as he kicks a paint can that's been left by the living room door, a fraction of a second too late, he realises the lid was only placed on top, not sealed. "No, no, no, no ..." Dave cries as the can topples and magnolia paint spills onto the new carpet in the living room and hallway. He scrambles to pick it up and limit the damage, almost dropping his phone as he does so.

He casts his eyes around for some rags or dust sheets, anything he can use to mop up the paint. Throwing a couple of old towels down as a start, he's frantically searching on Google for "How to get paint out of carpet ..." An hour later, Dave wants to scream. He's pretty sure the carpet is beyond saving. "I haven't got the money to replace it," he thinks, well aware that he's at the top end of his refurbishment budget as it is.

****

Ibrahim parks a few doors down from number 5 Parkland Drive. As he walks up the road, he can see his project manager Phil standing on the new driveway, talking animatedly to (Ibrahim assumes) one of the contractors. Phil catches sight of Ibrahim and gives him a wave, exiting his conversation. "Ibrahim, hi, great to see you. We're really excited to show you all the progress we've made." Ibrahim beams, "I'm excited to see it!"

"There is just one thing that Mo, our plumber and heating engineer, has just flagged up though, and I'm afraid it's not the best news ..." Ibrahim waits for Phil to continue. "So, the boiler isn't in as great a shape as we thought and for the amount it will cost to repair it, he reckons you're better off just installing a new boiler," Phil waits for Ibrahim's reaction.

His brow furrows slightly as he does his mental calculations. "Did Mo give a quote for a new boiler?" Ibrahim asks. "Yes, he thinks it'll be £1,200 all-in," Phil replies, still looking slightly worried. Ibrahim nods, "I've allowed a bit for contingency, so that should be fine, and it's another selling point for the property when all's said and done," Ibrahim says.

"Oh, great," Phil replies, visibly relieved. "In that case, let's go and look at the rest of the house and we can sort out the details for the boiler later."

As Ibrahim pulls out from Parkland Drive, he feels confident that it's all progressing as he'd hoped. The house is looking great and he's going to have to thank Salma for her input on the paint colours – the pale terracotta wall in the living room really does make it feel like a much more welcoming and friendly space. Even the need for a new boiler can't dampen his spirits – Ibrahim allowed an additional £1,500 over his £15,000 budget – but Phil has done a great job and has even managed to save him some money by using the paving slabs from the patio in the back garden to create the new driveway out front.

Two weeks later, Ibrahim's phone rings. It's Suri, his letting agent. "Hi Mr Nahas, how are you today?" "Very well thank you Suri, what can I do for you?"

"I wanted to let you know that since we put the property on the market last week, we've had a lot of interest. I don't think there will be any trouble letting it for £1,000 a month. I'll send you the details, but there are two families who are particularly interested and who both want to view the property once the refurbishment is finished."

"Excellent!" Ibrahim exclaims. "We are on track to finish by Friday."

"Great news, I will see if I can book these viewings for the end of next week," Suri says, "Both of them were particularly pleased that you've got a private driveway at the house," she adds.

Ibrahim smiles as he hangs up the phone. He knew that providing parking would make a difference – that street is a nightmare for parking at times and all the houses with their own driveways seemed to rent and sell for higher amounts.

Due diligence is an essential first step before you invest in a property and it leads neatly into adding value. Within the anonymous landlord mindset, you have two parts: CEO and investor. The CEO aspect of the mindset is all about running your property investment as a business. The investor aspect is taking the emotion out of property and seeing it as an investment vehicle like any other.

With any investment vehicle, you want to add value – and property is no different. There are various ways you can achieve this, but first let's look at what I mean by "value".

WHAT IS VALUE?

Firstly, value does not necessarily mean how much a property is worth. Sure, you could buy a property for £100,000, refurbish it and then it is worth £150,000, but it's important to understand that property holds value in various ways.

The obvious definition of value is its direct sale value and, when that is higher than what you purchased it for (as in that brief example), it allows you to borrow more because the property is also more valuable to mortgage lenders. However, the value of your newly refurbished property comes through in other ways – it's more appealing to tenants, because it has recently been refurbished and it gives you a stronger exit strategy, because you'll be able to sell it more quickly if it's been done up.

In a nutshell, this property you bought for £100,000 has become more valuable as an investment because, once you've refurbished it, less can go wrong, there's less to maintain and repair, meaning it presents fewer risks.

It's also important to note that the term "refurbishment" can mean many different things to different people. It could simply be cosmetic – a new coat of paint and maybe a new kitchen and/or bathroom – or it could be a full renovation of the property. Personally, I define a standard refurbishment to include replacing the bathroom, kitchen and flooring, and decorating internally. As soon as you do anything more significant, like adding an extension, removing a wall, or converting the loft, it becomes a renovation project.

That's just how I distinguish between the two, so when I talk about a refurbishment throughout this chapter, what I've just outlined is what I have in mind. Ultimately all these activities, whether you call them refurbishments or renovations, do the same thing: add value.

As I've explained, value isn't just the sale price. A refurbishment might add no value to the property itself, but it might mean you can increase the rent you charge or the speed with which the property rents out.

The other way in which you can add value to your investment is to buy a property below the market value. So, if you bought a property worth £100,000 for £80,000, you've "added" £20,000 in value. That might sound silly, but as an investor, you've simply bought an asset for less than its standard market value and that has put more money in your pocket.

DIFFERENT APPROACHES TO ADDING VALUE

There are different approaches you can take to adding value. None of these are right or wrong – which one works for you will depend on your goal for your investment.

In my experience, there are two typical routes that landlords take when it comes to adding value and investing. The first is to invest a lump sum of cash (let's say £100,000) in a property, to rent it out and then collect the income. For these landlords, it's a single investment and they have no desire to expand and run a larger portfolio.

The second are people who want to use that same lump sum of cash to build a property portfolio over the course of the next ten years. For these investors, adding value to a property and getting cash out of it quickly will be the name of the game, because this will give them the capital to grow their portfolio.

However, notice that both of these people are taking a long-term approach to their investments. Their goals are different, but they have this in common. So, the first landlord's goal might simply be to rent the property and use that rent to pay off the mortgage. The second landlord's goal, on the other hand, might be to build a portfolio and keep investing until they have £100,000 a year of profits coming in.

There are also many ways in which you can add value to a property investment. These include:

- Refurbishments, which can increase the value of the property (but not always) or simply make it easier to rent a property.

- Renovations, which will likely increase the value of the property and rent, as well as make it easier to rent.

- Converting a loft space into another bedroom, which will inevitably increase the value of the property and the rent.

- Extend the property, such as by building a kitchen-diner at the back of the house.

- Convert a forecourt to a driveway, which means you're adding a feature like parking.

- Convert a house into two flats.

- Convert a house into an HMO (let it out room by room).

- Convert flats or houses into serviced accommodation, short-term lets or holiday lets.

- Convert commercial properties into residential properties.

MY FAVOURITE WAY TO ADD VALUE

My personal favourite option when it comes to adding value to property is a standard refurbishment. I buy a house, replace the kitchen, bathroom and flooring and redecorate. It's one of the lowest-risk options, it's quick, it's easy and, in my opinion, is the best in terms of how much you spend versus how much you increase the value of your investment.

Compare that to a complete restructure of a property where you knock walls down, move things around and so on. In this scenario, I could buy a property for £100,000, spend £100,000 on the restructure and end up with a property worth £300,000, but that takes a huge amount of time, there's a lot that could go wrong and I have to put in a lot of cash. That's not to say I wouldn't do that, but for the most part I prefer the low risk, high return of a standard refurbishment.

IDENTIFYING YOUR PROPERTY INVESTMENT GOAL

My team all use a handy acronym that I've come up with – TOM (which I love because it also happens to be my name). TOM stands for target, objective and methods.

TARGET: your target doesn't need to be longer than one or two sentences that set out your ultimate goal from your property investment. It can be monetary or something else. For example, you might have a target of ten properties, £5,000 per month profit or £1,000,000 of equity.

OBJECTIVES: these are the individual objectives and milestones you need to hit in order to achieve your target.

METHOD: this is the task list – or to-do list – you need to follow in order to achieve each objective.

LANDLORD NUMBER 1

TARGET: *I have £100,000 of cash sitting in the bank and I want to invest it for a good return on investment through monthly cash flow.*

OBJECTIVES: *I can buy a property for up to £350,000; I'll need to get £1,500 per month in rent; I'll need to get a mortgage for £x (and so on).*

METHOD: *I must have a lettings agent, a solicitor, and a mortgage broker to help me achieve my objectives.*

LANDLORD NUMBER 2

TARGET: *I have £100,000 of cash sitting in the bank and I want to invest in property to build a portfolio of properties.*

OBJECTIVES: *I can buy a property for up to £300,000; I'll need to refurbish it for £10,000; I'll need to get £1,500 per month in rent and have reliable tenants; I'll need to get a mortgage for £x; I'll need to refinance that mortgage in two year's time to take capital out to invest in my next property.*

METHOD: *I must have a lettings agent, contractors, a solicitor, and a mortgage broker to help me achieve my objectives. I must also set up a limited company to run this as a business.*

When you are thinking about how best to add value to your property investments, start with your target. By the way, if you're going to set yourself a target, make it awesome! Go for it. When you know what you want to achieve, it is much easier to find the best steps to take along the way towards your target.

As I've said, neither of these approaches is right or wrong – both of these people can be anonymous landlords. What you have to decide is where your comfort zone is and what you need to do to achieve your target. You can buy lots of properties to begin with or you can focus on taking on one project at a time. I've done both ways and both have their challenges.

If you take on one project at a time, you might be frustrated with how long it takes to grow your portfolio. I was. However, then I bought multiple properties all at the same time and became frustrated with trying to coordinate all the purchases and projects. Having said this, I then improved my business operation so I was less involved; but when you're buying a property, you will inevitably be involved and you'll have to handle some parts of the purchase.

If refinancing every couple of years and having maxed-out mortgages is only going to stress you out, don't do it. Think carefully about your goals and use them to determine your approach to property investment.

The top investors in the world try to leverage mortgages in order to make more monthly cash flow, buy more properties and maximise their equity. However, some people don't share this mentality and never will. There's no point in leveraging mortgages if you're going to be constantly uncomfortable.

BUDGETING FOR ADDING VALUE

With the exception of buying a property for below its market value, you will need to spend some money in order to add value to your investment. The key is, naturally, to ensure you're not spending more than the value you're adding.

My general rule is not to spend more than 75 per cent of the amount of increased value that you're going to achieve. So, if you are doing work to add £10,000 to the value of a property, spend £7,500 or less on that project. This is a really simple but effective way of calculating your initial budget for a refurbishment or any other work you're undertaking.

The reason I recommend not spending more than 75 per cent of the value added is that, in most cases, you can only borrow up to 75 per cent of the value of a property. Let's say you purchase a property for £100,000 and, once you've accounted for all of your fees, taxes and the refurbishment, the project costs £120,000 in total. Having done that work, the property is now worth £150,000 and you can refinance or remortgage 75 per cent of that amount, allowing you to take £112,500 back out of the property. This amount will pay off the original mortgage. That means you're leaving £7,500 in this particular property investment.

You might not mind leaving some money in a property investment. Personally, I don't mind leaving £10,000 in a property provided it is delivering a good yield (this is why calculating your yield is so important before you make the purchase, because it will affect how you budget for adding value). So, if I leave £10,000 of my cash in a particular property, but it's generating £5,000 a year in net profit, that means all my cash is paid back within two years. Thereafter, that £5,000 is pure profit because I've got all the cash back I initially invested.

DON'T CHASE UNICORNS, BUY A WORKHORSE

Although the ideal when you're adding value to a property investment is to get as much of your cash out of it as possible, I would caution you against searching for what I call a unicorn property, which is one that will pay back all of your cash investment on day one. Firstly, there are very few, if any, properties that can deliver that kind of return. Secondly, everybody is looking for them; and thirdly, it takes a great deal of time and energy to find one (if you ever do).

Workhorses, on the other hand, are plentiful. These are the kinds of properties I described in that previous example, where you're able to get your cash back within a few years and the property delivers a high yield and therefore good profits. The problem with chasing unicorns is that you'll miss the workhorses. If you spend a year searching for a unicorn, and in that time you let ten workhorses slide by, you've lost out.

WAITING IS EXPENSIVE

I first met Raj when he had a "discovery call" with me – this is what I have with potential investors who want help finding the right properties. I gave him some ideas (everything I've already told you!) – look for a PRESS property, build a solid base of PRESS properties first and then you will have profit to invest in more adventurous properties later. Raj told me he wanted to do a flip to double his cash so he could get more properties faster. That's how we left it.

A year later, he contacted me saying he'd not yet found a property and asked if I could help him find one. He said he'd made loads of offers but nobody had accepted. When he talked me through a few examples I could see why! He was offering low to try and make a load of profit. As a result, the agents stopped inviting him to viewings and he was not being taken seriously. It's frustrating for an agent to keep having to present silly offers to their customers. I told Raj two things ...

Firstly, if you're set on doing a flip, set your sights a little lower. Try to get a "good deal" instead of a "unicorn deal". By this I meant instead of trying to make £60,000 in one flip deal, find three deals that make you £20,000 each. They're easier to find, less risky and faster. A big flip which will make you £60,000 will come with major increased risk – more can go wrong on a huge refurb – not to mention that you're unlikely to get someone to accept a silly offer and you'll make a bad name for yourself as an investor. When you get labelled as a greedy investor who just makes silly offers, nobody will want to serve you. Plus, why would someone offer you a deal where you can make £60k?? They'd do it themselves, right?

Secondly, you've had your cash sitting in the bank for 12 months to try and make an extra profit on a flip. In that time, you could have generated £10,000 in rent, £10,000 in appreciation and, if you'd done it properly, you could also have added value to the property which would have given you most (or all) of your cash back through refinancing. Instead, you've been trying to find the unicorn deal (which are super-rare) and you've still not got one.

You could end up waiting another year to get one with no guarantee you'll even find one. You've also ruined your reputation, you've wasted TONS of your time on viewings and searching, AND you've also lost money.

During that 12 months, inflation means your initial £200,000 is now worth less – 12 months ago, your £200,000 would have bought you 200,000 loaves of bread, 2,000 tanks of fuel, or a three-bedroom house. It's now 12 months later, you STILL have £200,000 but it will now only buy you 180,000 loaves of bread, 1,800 tanks of fuel, or a two-bedroom house. This is an extreme example but the maths is accurate – waiting is expensive!

It's important to manage your expectations and not set unrealistic goals for your property investments. There are many training courses available that pedal the myth of the "£1 property" or the "all money out" deals. Or there are coaches and trainers who make borrowing £120,000 sound easy. I can tell you now, it's not (and finding a £1 property is like catching a herd of unicorns). It has taken me 20 years to reach a point where lenders are happy to lend me large sums of cash. I certainly didn't have access to that kind of finance when I was starting out.

I'm sure you can see how easy it would be to get sucked into chasing those unicorns, and this is why it's so important to have a system and the right mindset when it comes to adding value to property investments.

The reason those training programmes I mentioned are so effective is that they make property investing emotional. It's easy to see those headlines and think, "So if I've got £10,000 cash, you mean I can get a property for free and get my £10,000 back!" That's an emotional feeling, it's not logical at all.

However, the anonymous landlord, as you know, doesn't view property as an emotional investment. It's logical all the way. That's why the calculation to set your budget for adding value is so useful. If you do want to get all the money you spend back on a property investment quickly, you will ruthlessly stick to that 75 per cent budget. However, if, like me, you are comfortable leaving some money in a property, your budget will be the amount you are happy to leave in that property.

By focusing on the figures and budgeting, you remove the emotion from your decisions and will be able to spot the workhorse properties by doing the financial calculations I discussed in the previous chapter as part of your due diligence.

By the way, I am definitely NOT saying that unicorn properties don't exist. They really do exist if you can find them. I have completed a few of these unicorn projects myself. The point I'm trying to get across is that I've been in the industry for years, built up tons of contacts and I still find it hard to get these deals. So I don't wait around for them. If I get one, I'll buy it but I certainly won't miss out on 25 per cent yields or more because I'm waiting for a better deal.

SET A PERCENTAGE RETURN, RATHER THAN A FINANCIAL FIGURE

I often get asked how much property investors can realistically expect as an annual return, on average; and if you're talking in figures that's an impossible question to answer because of the geographical variations between property markets in the UK.

My advice is to set your TOM and have your target to achieve a minimum return on your cash, such as a ten per cent return on your cash which is very realistic and common. That means if you have to use £50,000 of your money to buy a house worth £200,000, you want to make £5,000 in net profit every year, which is certainly achievable.

The higher the yield, the harder they are to find and the fewer properties there are to choose from. Most of the wealthiest people I know have said the words, "I just want ten per cent return on all my cash." That's because those properties are easy to find, easy to buy, and fast to turn into profit.

Personally, I don't look at properties that give me less than 20 per cent return on the cash I have left in that property. So, if I've got £10,000 in a property, I want it to be delivering a minimum of £2,000 in net profits. This is because I've been involved in property for many years and I know how to find these properties. It's how I source and broker loads of properties to my clients too. I've built this network of property people over many years.

There are also regions of the UK where I'd see an eight per cent return as very reasonable, because of the nature of those particular markets. The key is to research the market you intend to buy in, find out what's possible and set your target from there.

Once you've set your target return, it's your job to maintain that percentage. Let's stick with the example of investing £50,000 and looking for £5,000 a year back. If mortgage interest rates go up, or expenditure goes up elsewhere, you have to increase rents or reduce expenditure to maintain your ten per cent return. Alternatively, if the rental market where your property is located drops dramatically for some reason (and doesn't look like it will recover quickly), you may decide to sell that property and buy another one that can easily deliver you a ten per cent return.

Approaching your property investments through this lens again helps to keep the emotion out of your decisions and instead means you make logical decisions based on your goals as an investor and the state of the market. Remember that there is always huge demand for property, so far from being trapped once you purchase a property, you actually have a lot of control. You keep it until you decide to sell it.

The main goal here is not about the property: it's about the return on your cash, or your cash yield. Sometimes selling a property in order to reinvest is the right move. It's not about the property. You're an investor – your job is to invest, and all investing is supposed to pro-duce the right yield.

One final point on the returns your property generates is to make sure you have a long-term target, as well as a short-term objective for your returns. So, your short-term objective could be to make a ten per cent return on your cash investment each year. However, your long-term target return on investment is a 100 per cent return over a ten-year period. That means if one year you don't make your ten per cent, you can hold onto that property if you believe it will make more than that the following year. There are no guarantees with any investing so you have to take a long-term view. Some years you'll make more, some years you'll make less.

You might see a market dip which means your short-term return falls to, let's say, eight per cent. However, if the following year your return rebounds to 14 per cent, you're more than back on track. The key, as always, is not to get emotional because this is when it becomes easy to panic about a downturn and make choices that ultimately mean you lose out. Always stay logical.

If you have bought a property with the intention of keeping it for ten, 15 or even 20 years (as most property investors do), there's no need to worry if its value drops in the first year or two. The important thing is to keep an eye on its performance and make sure it's still aligned to your ten-year target.

ALWAYS REMEMBER WHY YOU'VE INVESTED IN PROPERTY

When you're setting budgets for adding value to your property, it can be very easy to fall into the trap of thinking, "If I do the decorating myself, I'll save X amount ..." But I would urge you to remember why you are investing in property and to come back to the pots of profit I talked about in Chapter 1.

If you truly enjoy stripping walls and painting, then by all means do this yourself. However, never do these jobs with the mindset of saving money. I know too many people who do this, and underestimate the work involved. They buy a property and think they'll do it up in the evenings on and on weekends, around their full-time job. One month down the line, they're tired, things have gone wrong, and they're realising they should have just got someone else to do the work.

Remember the old adage "buy cheap, buy twice" – it's the same if you try to refurbish a property yourself to save money. Don't cut corners and instead budget for having professionals to do the refurbishment work for you. I know so many landlords and property investors who have chosen to do the work themselves and have not done the work to the right standard. It ends up costing more time, money and effort. Poor work makes letting a property more difficult too.

Before you decide to do any work yourself, think about why you got into property investing. Was it to become a painter/decorator? If the answer is no, then don't do it! As I said in Chapter 1, there's no point in having a full cash pot if your time, energy, family and mental health pots are all empty. You've got to keep all of your pots full, and sometimes that means spending a bit of cash to make sure you're not depleting all the others.

USE THE PRESS TEST

The PRESS test I outlined in relation to due diligence can also be applied to adding value. Whether you're thinking of carrying out a standard refurbishment or converting a property, apply the PRESS test before you commit to anything.

PROFITABLE: will it be profitable? For example, is the cost of the work going to be less than 75 per cent of the increase in value?

RELIABLE: is it a reliable way to generate the return you want? For example, how sure are you that the value will increase by your expectation? Try and value it again using a worst-case scenario.

EASY: is it easy to do? Easy in – easy out. Will this work make it easy to exit from, if you need to, and are you increasing demand for tenants moving in?

SIMPLE: is it a simple process or is this going to be a complicated project? Keep it simple. The simplest projects are normally the best.

SAFE: does this make a safer investment? Have you calculated the worst-case scenarios and risks?

For a standard refurbishment, I can confidently say it meets the PRESS test. If I budget correctly, it will be profitable. I know from experience that it's a reliable way to increase the value of a property. There are thousands of kitchen and bathroom fitters available, so it's easy. It's also very simple because it's one of the most common refurbishments you can do, and it's safe because you're not building or demolishing anything.

A property conversion, on the other hand, might be profitable and reliable, but it is unlikely to be easy or simple and it carries a much higher risk, so it's not necessarily safe either.

"Remember that property holds value in many ways;
it's not all about the resale value."

ANONYMOUS LANDLORD ACTION POINT

Work through the TOM acronym for your next property investment. Write out your target, objectives and method.

6 SECURING FINANCE

Dave sighs as he scans over the mortgage statement for his buy-to-let property. The rent is covering all his costs, including the mortgage, and leaving him with a small profit, but it's not as much as he'd hoped to get. He spoke to Suri last week about the possibility of increasing the rent, but she'd advised him against it. His phone buzzes, "Fancy a pint?" Dom always seems to know when he's fed up with property admin. He replies with a thumbs up and gets ready to go, happy to leave his financial deliberations for another day.

"You didn't waste any time," Dom says when he sees Dave at the bar, already one-third of the way through his first pint. Dave grins sheepishly, "Anything to get away from mortgage statements," he says.

"For the rental property?" Dom inquires.

"Yeah, I've been trying to work out how I can squeeze a bit more profit from it."

"Refinance?" Dom asks. "Maybe, just not sure where to start with all that. Might need to pay a mortgage broker, but I don't really want to add another expense into the mix," Dave explains.

"Might be worth it though, if it saves you in the long term?" Dave nods, he has to admit that Dom makes a very good point.

One week later, he's meeting with a mortgage adviser. "How long have you owned your buy-to-let property Mr Keenan?" "About a year." "Great, and it's reliably rented?" Dave nods.

"I think I can certainly beat the rate you're on at the moment, as it's not particularly competitive, especially in the current market," Sam explains.

Dave smiles, "I mean, that would be great. I just went to my bank in the first instance as it seemed the simplest thing to do."

Sam nods, "Of course, leave it with me and I'll get back to you with some offers within a week."

****

Ibrahim idly taps his fingers on his desk as he waits for the Zoom call to connect. Eventually his video flickers to life and he's facing Sam, his mortgage broker. "Mr Nahas, lovely to see you again. Just remind me what you'd like to go over today?"

"As you know, I've been renting my property for just over three months, having refurbished it, but I'd like to refinance so I can get some of my capital out and build my property portfolio."

Sam nods, "Of course. Have you had the property valued since you completed the refurbishment?"

"I have indeed," Ibrahim says. "I paid £165,000 for it and, according to the valuations I've had this month, it is now worth £205,000."

"That's great news!" Sam says, "Sounds like you've done really well with that one." Ibrahim nods in acknowledgement, "Well, I got a good deal in the first place as the seller wanted a quick sale and it didn't take much research to see what needed doing to make it stand out from some of the others on that street.

"I've already asked my bank what rate they'd give me on the property," Ibrahim adds. "I'll email you the particulars, but I think you might be able to do better." Sam nods, "Sure, send their offer over and I'll see what I can do!"

Ibrahim and Sam spend the next half hour looking at the current mortgage and calculating how much Ibrahim will be able to take out of the property by refinancing. By the end of the call, Sam has promised to get back to him within the week with the best mortgage deals he can find on the market. As Ibrahim clicks "Leave call" he checks his watch – ten minutes until his next meeting, this time with Melanie to see if she can find him another property to invest in.

There are many myths around securing finance for property investments, as well as a few very simple steps you can take that will help you on your journey to becoming an anonymous landlord (but these are steps most people won't tell you about).

In the last chapter, I mentioned the property training programmes that are advertised with headlines like, "Find out how to buy a property for just £1", "No Money Down", and "Get a House for Free". I understand the marketing tactics they're employing, but this has resulted in many people having unrealistic expectations about the kinds of property deals they can find.

As I said, don't chase unicorns, buy workhorses! I'm not saying you can't get a property with those tactics, I'm saying you can't buy a property for £1. Well, you can't in the normal world of property anyway – the way it sounds is not the way it actually is.

WHAT "BUY A PROPERTY FOR £1" *REALLY* MEANS

So, can you really buy a property for £1? If you think that means you just need £1 to invest, then no. This is how these deals usually work:

You buy a property for £100,000.

↓

You refurbish it for £20,000.

↓

With all the fees and stamp duty etc., the total cost is £130,000.

BUT it's now worth £175,000 because you've "added value".

↓

You refinance, taking out a new mortgage of £130,000, which pays off the original purchase mortgage.

↓

You've got all your cash back AND you own the house which is rented out.

This is what I call a Flip to Let. Often these deals are called BRRR (buy, refurbish, rent, refinance). These are the deals that are sometimes advertised as "get a free property" or "get a house for £1". You technically don't get a free house – you still need the cash to invest in the first place and you're technically without that cash for eight months while you do all this.

These are also unicorn deals. They're extremely rare!

A more common and reliable form of BRRR is where you might not get ALL your cash back out through the refinance. Instead, you might leave £10,000, £20,000 (or whatever) in the property as equity. This means, in the above example, instead of the property being worth £175,000 when you've finished the refurb, it's now worth £165,000. So, you get a lot of your money back but not quite all of it. You still own that cash as equity but it's just not back in your bank. I do these deals A LOT.

Why is not chasing unicorns important in relation to securing finance? Because when you buy a workhorse you can start making money straight away. That doesn't mean you have to stop searching for unicorns – if you're lucky enough to stumble on one, you can always sell your workhorse (which should be relatively easy to do if you've followed my advice around due diligence and adding value) and buy the unicorn.

By the way, a unicorn is that dream property investment that produces HUGE, life-changing profits. A workhorse is the normal, realistic property investment that produces a good return on investment but probably won't make you a millionaire by the end of the month.

If your money is just sitting in the bank while you're searching for that miraculous deal, however, it's not working for you and you could be waiting a very long time until you find one. In fact, in most examples your money is decreasing in value while it's sitting in the bank.

This might be something you've heard about before but let me explain. If you have £100,000 sitting in your savings account today, you might be able to buy 100,000 loaves of bread for £1 each. Easy enough. However, in two years time, each loaf of bread will cost £1.10. Therefore, in two years time, your £100,000 can only buy 91,000 loaves of bread. That's a lot of carbs! Anyway, this is "inflation" in its basic form – the cost of stuff.

It's also likely that your bank will be paying you 0.0000000000000000055 per year in interest which you probably won't even notice. OK, that's an exaggeration, but you get my point. So, the value of your money sitting in the bank is decreasing all the time. By this logic, you'd be better off investing in an investment property that produces a two per cent return on investment than you are leaving the money in your bank doing nothing other than decreasing in value.

OK, OK, I haven't factored in the risk here. You could invest your money into something and end up losing money – but hopefully, with the right due-diligence and with the right people and companies supporting you, these risks can be seriously minimised.

So, top tip number one (although not strictly related to securing finance) is to invest in a property as soon as you find one that ticks all your boxes and that will deliver your target, rather than waiting for "the perfect opportunity" to appear on Rightmove (I can tell you now, it won't!).

Those unicorn properties very rarely make it to the open market and, if they do, you can guarantee you'll be up against tons of other investors. That means you'll either miss it, you'll get outbid, or the bidding war increases the purchase price to a point where it stops being a unicorn deal and becomes a workhorse anyway. What do I mean? If you do manage to spot a unicorn deal online for £150,000 and you've worked out that you can get 20 per cent return on your investment – WOW! However, you can guarantee that many other investors have seen it too.

When there is a good property investment, there will be lots of interest and lots of offers. When lots of people offer on a property, it will turn into a bidding war because that's the estate agent's job. Remember, the agent doesn't work for the buyer, they work for the seller. The agent's job is to get as much money for the seller as possible, as quickly as possible.

So, when you get into a bidding war, inevitably the purchase price will go up and you might end up paying £165,000 rather than the £150,000 you initially saw it for. Now it's not a unicorn property with a 20 per cent ROI, it's a workhorse property with a ten per cent ROI. You could have been waiting for this unicorn property for 12 months, which means you've missed out on 12 months of rent, 12 months of adding value, 12 months of return on your investment. Oh, and you've probably lost some money because your cash was sitting in the bank for 12 months. OUCH!

TOP TIP #1: Invest right now, because some profit is better than no profit.

FINANCING YOUR PROPERTY INVESTMENT

One of the biggest myths surrounding property investment is that you need to be a cash buyer to become a property investor, or you need tons of cash. This is simply not true. In fact, in many cases you can make a higher cash yield as an investor if you buy a property with a mortgage, because you're putting less of your own cash into the property.

Of course, this depends on many factors such as: interest rates, purchase prices, rent values, and so on. The point is, it's not always logical to buy with cash, you don't always need tons of cash to invest, and you also don't need a crystal clear credit rating either.

This section will give you some ideas for financing purchases, refinancing properties, and using mortgage lenders. It will also give you some fundamental information about how the financial services work. I genuinely believe it's important for a property investor and landlord to understand how the mortgage world works from all perspectives.

A buy-to-let mortgage is the most common way of funding a property investment. Many people will do one of two things: they'll go straight to their bank or they'll go straight to a mortgage broker – very few people will go to both. This is a huge mistake that many property investors make.

My advice is to start by approaching your bank. As you're an existing customer, they may offer you a preferential rate, particularly if you have a good history with them. Once you have a mortgage approval and a quote from your bank, go to a mortgage broker and ask if they can find a lender that will beat what your bank is offering you. A mortgage broker will look at all the lenders on the market to find the best deal available to you. Usually they'll be able to tell you very quickly whether they can find a better deal for you and that costs nothing.

I would also advise going to a mortgage broker that specialises in buy-to-let mortgages. Loads of mortgage advisers will hate me for saying that but it's like most professions – you can work with a "Jack of all trades" or you can work with a specialist who focuses on the actual service you need. Personally, I prefer a specialist.

I used to be a mortgage adviser and I can tell you, the investment mortgage world is very different to the residential mortgage world. I have also been in property for a very, very, very long time and I've worked with all types of mortgage advisers. I think I'm reasonably qualified to advise you to find a specialist mortgage adviser.

If you arrange a mortgage through a broker, you may have to pay a fee, but it will usually only be a couple of hundred pounds and if they find you a mortgage that saves you money per month, that will pay for itself very quickly.

Some mortgage brokers don't charge a fee but personally, I never try to buy "cheap" when it comes to important services. You know what they say: buy cheap, buy twice. If, on the other hand, it turns out your bank is offering the best rate, you can go directly to them and it won't have cost anything other than a bit of your time. The point is to use the resources available to you in order to secure the absolute best mortgage deal you can.

When you're looking for a buy-to-let mortgage as a new (or relatively new) property investor, it's important to remember you're buying a set product and there is little to no room for negotiation. As you go further on your journey as an anonymous landlord, you may develop relationships with specialist lenders that will enable you to create bespoke products that offer you better rates. This is the kind of arrangement I have with various lenders now, but it has taken me years to reach this point. In some cases, I've been pre-approved so I don't need to apply for mortgages anymore.

When you start out, the most important thing to consider is which mortgage deal will deliver you a profit, and you have to take the best that you can get on the open market. The best advice I can give you is to assess the market thoroughly by going to your bank *and* seeing a mortgage broker.

**TOP TIP #2: Get a specialist mortgage broker AND get a quote from your own bank.
Then compare the options.**

DIFFERENT TYPES OF LENDERS

Mainstream banks are the most obvious lenders, which is most likely who you bank with and therefore where you'll start your search for a buy-to-let mortgage. In addition to these institutions, there are also mortgage lenders that only lend mortgages and don't offer any other products like current or savings accounts. Finally, there are specialist mortgage lenders that will offer mortgages specifically for investment such as buy-to-let, bridging finance and development finance. There are also some specialist lenders that specialise in properties that are being purchased below market value.

When you're looking for finance for property investments, the key is to compare the products on offer across the whole market, not just with the high street banks that you're familiar with. Again, this is where a mortgage broker is very useful, because they will know about these alternative lenders and can point you in their direction. You can also do this yourself if you're prepared to invest the time and energy into it. Personally, I'd just pay my specialist mortgage broker to do that for me. That's why I'm an anonymous landlord, I suppose.

DIFFERENT FINANCE OPTIONS

The most obvious way to finance a property investment is with a buy-to-let mortgage. These are usually the best option if the property you're buying is habitable and ready to rent out (or even already tenanted). You can, of course, pay for a property in cash, but as I mentioned earlier that may not be the best option.

Bridging loans are another form of finance that you can consider. These aren't mortgages but are short-term loans secured against the property and they're typically used when you're buying an uninhabitable property that needs refurbishment. As the name suggests, this finance "bridges the gap" between the purchase of the property and you taking out a mortgage.

A bridging loan is useful to give you the funds to buy the property and the time to refurbish a property, but it is only short-term finance and will need to be replaced with a buy-to-let mortgage as soon as the property can be lived in. Normally a bridging loan has a much higher interest rate than a mortgage because it's usually paid off within a year.

Cash, as I've mentioned, is your other finance option. You may decide to purchase a rundown property with cash, renovate it and then mortgage it once it's habitable, removing the need for a bridging loan. Having said that, I know some seriously wealthy people who buy all their properties with cash. I also know some seriously wealthy people who only buy properties with mortgages.

It's not always about the profit you can generate. It's also about your preferences and comfort zones. If you're more comfortable paying cash and you really don't want to use mortgages, do what you feel is best for you. There's no point making more profit because you've leveraged mortgages if you're going to spend the next 25 years uncomfortable with your investments. Remember, your cash pot is just one of your pots. Don't take anything out of your mental wellbeing pot just to put more in your cash pot.

CHANGING YOUR MINDSET AROUND MORTGAGES

A lot of people think that mortgages are for buying properties, but at their most basic level they are about borrowing against the value of an asset (which in this case happens to be a property).

That means if you buy a property for £100,000 cash, refurbish it and bring its value up to £150,000, that you can then get a mortgage and borrow up to £112,500 (or 75 per cent of its value). This new mortgage will pay off any loan you took on to buy the property and gives you some or all of your cash investment back. Taking your cash out of the property enables you to go again and find the next property. Of course, when you take out a mortgage you pay interest on your repayments, so you need to factor that in.

However, if you do the maths you will usually find that, even with the interest payments, taking out a mortgage for a property investment is the most cost-effective way to finance it. Let's look at an example to demonstrate what I mean.

I'm going to assume you're starting with £100,000 for these examples. You can adjust the calculations to match the amount of cash you'd be starting with. I'm also going to ignore things like stamp duty, legal fees etc. I'm also not going into tax as everyone's tax position will be different.

So, if you buy a property for £100,000 with your own cash and you're receiving £500 per month in rent (after your other costs), that money is pretty much all yours, because you don't have to repay a mortgage. That equates to £6,000 per year or a six per cent cash yield. Therefore, you have £100,000 of your own cash invested in this property and that cash investment is generating £6,000 per year in profit. That's a cash yield of six per cent.

Let's look at how that stacks up if you buy that same property with a mortgage of £75,000.

Your cash investment is £25,000 of your own money because you're only putting down a deposit. You're still receiving £500 per month in rent, but you have to pay £200 per month on your mortgage interest. That leaves you with a profit of £300 per month, or £3,600 per year. But, it also means you've only used £25,000 of your cash to buy the property. Therefore, your cash investment is £25,000 which is producing a profit of £3,600 per year. That means your cash yield is around 14.5 per cent.

However, let's now imagine that you buy four properties. You'll use £25,000 of your own cash as a deposit for each one (because you started with £100,000 to invest). You'll take a £75,000 mortgage on each one. These four properties will generate £2,000 in rent and you're paying mortgage payments of £1,200 (£300 each property). This means that for the same £100,000, you're earning £14,400 per year profit, which is considerably more than the £6,000 you get for owning one property that you bought with cash. It's more than double!

There is something of a stigma around mortgages in the UK, which is an emotional reaction for some people. However, as you know, the key to becoming an anonymous landlord is to take the emotion out of situations and rely on logic. Logically, owning properties with mortgages can give you a higher yield and therefore a higher profit – it's the emotional desire to avoid having multiple mortgages that holds some property investors back. It's important to focus on the logical side of investing so you are investing for the right reasons.

> **TOP TIP #3: Do the maths. Stick to the maths. Trust the maths – often taking out mortgages on multiple properties will deliver better returns than only owning and renting one property that's mortgage free.**

MORE PROPERTIES = LESS RISK

Emotion is one of the biggest challenges property investors face and it's fears arising from emotions that hold many people back from becoming anonymous landlords. Sometimes we don't realise that we're being driven and influenced by our emotions. Some people don't accept that they're making emotional decisions.

The important thing to remember is what "emotion" means. It's not a weakness. It doesn't make you less of a person. In fact, the best property investors and most successful people on the planet accept and understand their emotions, and ensure their minds are strong enough to make logical decisions. One of the most common worries is that, if the property market crashes and you hold multiple properties, you'll lose everything.

I'd like to address this myth head on. Firstly, a property market crash won't reduce the value of houses to £0 because everyone needs somewhere to live. Yes, there could be a scenario where 25 per cent of the value is wiped out, but that is extremely unlikely and, if you're in it for the long term, values will recover if you hold out because they always have. Ask yourself the question, "What will this house be worth in 20 years?"

Secondly, holding more properties can actually minimise your risk in a lot of cases, rather than increasing it. Let me explain ...

You can be pretty sure that there is a five per cent risk of your tenant falling into arrears. This means that you will have a tenant that falls into arrears at least once every 25 years. This risk increases with certain tenants, certain properties, certain areas and certain demographics.

If you own one property and your tenants stop paying rent, that is all your income gone. If you've got four properties and one of your tenants stops paying rent, that's 1/4 of your income gone and the other three will still produce income to cover it. When you have multiple properties, they can cover an empty property and ensure that you're still making an income. This is a good way to spread your risk.

You can further mitigate your risk by buying properties in different locations, so that if the value of properties in one location falls, the others could still be growing in value. Similarly, if your aim is to grow a property portfolio, lenders will see you as less of a risk because you have more security and assets.

Let's imagine two of your friends from the pub ask if they can borrow £1,000 each. One says, "You can have my car until I pay it back." The other says, "I'm good for it, trust me ...". You're more comfortable with the more secure option. It's the same for mortgage lenders. The more security you have, the more they want to lend to you.

The bottom line is that the more properties you have, the more profit you'll have to cover everything from a void period to a boiler replacement.

Similarly, if you were to invest your entire £100,000 in a single property without a mortgage, this can be a higher-risk investment because if something goes seriously wrong with that property, you could lose a substantial amount of your money. If, on the other hand, you have £25,000 in that property and the rest is mortgaged, the remainder of your cash is protected or employed elsewhere.

Think about it logically – if you were investing in shares, you wouldn't put your entire £100,000 in just one company, you'd spread it out between the top performing companies on the stock market.

TOP TIP #4: Mitigate your risk by spreading it. Multiple properties in good locations will reduce your risk.

THINK LIKE AN ANONYMOUS LANDLORD

Removing the emotion from your property investing is one of the fundamentals of the anonymous landlord mindset, and it's one you need to master if you want to have a portfolio of properties because managing them all yourself isn't practical or advisable – certainly not if you're still in the traditional landlord mindset.

I've talked about financial risk, but there is also a risk that you'll fall foul of compliance if you try to do everything yourself, rather than getting support and becoming an anonymous landlord. If you've got ten properties, there's also a greater risk of all your time and energy going into managing them, rather than getting to spend that with your family, friends or doing what you enjoy.

As a DIY landlord, you're increasing your stress and your level of responsibility – often to unmanageable levels – once you own more than just one or two properties. When you become an anonymous landlord and put the right people and systems in place (which I'll talk about in Part 3) you reduce your stress and responsibility, while giving yourself more energy and time. Remember all those pots of profit. Money, time, energy, mind and family. Also, I said earlier that this isn't just about giving your property to a lettings agent to manage. That's just one way. You can also be an anonymous landlord as a DIY landlord.

In addition, as soon as you have multiple properties, it makes it easier for you to negotiate with letting agents over their fees, because they will be managing ten properties for you rather than just one or two. Dealing with just one client (you) for ten properties is less work for the letting agent, which may make them inclined to give you a discount on their services. Don't tell my lettings team that I've just offered a discount to every portfolio landlord that reads this book. Oops! Screw it, I'll just say it – if you mention that you've read this book, I'll give a discount to any landlord who wants to bring a letting agent on board. Shameless sales pitch – hope you don't mind!

This all comes back to the concept I shared at the beginning of the book, in that you need to treat being a landlord like being a business owner. You need to remove the emotion from the situation and think logically. If you look at all the world's biggest and most successful investors, you'll find that they approach any investment they make with logic. When it comes to property, that means using mortgages when you can and spreading the risk to your capital by investing in multiple assets.

DON'T LET FEES PUT YOU OFF

Part of being an anonymous landlord means using other people's expertise and skills to support you as a property investor, and you will have to pay for that expertise or those skills. All too often, people are put off by fees, but my advice to you is to look at the whole deal, rather than getting put off by parts of the deal.

You have to package the complete property investment deal into one figure, simplify it – all you need to know is how much it's going to cost you to complete the project and how much money you are going to get out of it. Don't worry about who you're going to be paying or how much, just focus on the deal as a whole. Cash investment and profit. That's it.

As an example, if I source an investment property for you, I'm going to ask for £3,000 for doing so. A lot of people will refuse to pay that, which they're entitled to do, but then they don't get the property. In this scenario, let's say you'll make £30,000 in profit from this property investment even after paying me the £3,000 – isn't that worth doing? Invest £3,000 to get £30,000. I'll take that.

My point is that it doesn't matter how much you end up paying if it's a good deal. Work out the cash in and cash out. It doesn't matter how much you're going to pay in fees – if the deal works, it works. For example, I've bought properties at auctions where the auction has charged five per cent of the purchase price. In some cases, that auction fee has been £7,500. That sounds ridiculous! But when you include that fee as part of the overall investment, it was a great deal.

THE BREAK DOWN OF A GREAT INVESTMENT DEAL

Purchase price: £151,000

Auction fee: five per cent (£7,550)

Refurbishment: £12,000

Stamp duty and other fees: £10,000

Cash employed: £30,000

End value: £225,000

New mortgage: £168,000

Cash working: £13,000

Rent profit: £500 per calendar month (£6,000 per year)

CASH YIELD: 46 PER CENT

Imagine getting a 46 per cent return each year on all your money! Would you care about paying a £7,550 auction fee if you saw that level of return? I think not!

It is very easy to get fixated on the "cost" element of a deal, but you really do have to look at the bigger picture logically (there's that word again!). Think about online shopping (and I'm sure you've done this), imagine there's a product for sale for £15 with free shipping. Brilliant, you're going to buy it. Now imagine that same product is for sale for £10 but shipping costs £4.99. I'm willing to bet you'd hesitate over buying it, or possibly even refuse to pay the shipping costs and therefore miss out on the purchase.

Within property, there are many fees that you have to pay and it's much easier to accept them if you just view them as part of the deal. Auction properties are a classic example and I've heard many people saying they won't buy at auction because of the fees, but what does that matter, really? Instead of thinking of them as separate, just incorporate them as part of the cost of buying a property when you're doing your budgeting and financial calculations. It's not about your feeling of value. It's about the actual and factual value; the actual and factual return on investment.

> **TOP TIP #5: Work out all the fees and costs as part of the investment. If it works, it works. If it doesn't, it doesn't. Don't miss out on deals because you hate paying fees.**

FOCUS ON YOUR LONG-TERM PLAN

When you start investing in property, it's essential that you set yourself a long-term target (remember TOM) and that you stick to it. If your ten-year plan is to generate £10,000 of profit per month from property so that you can give your family a comfortable life and financial security, don't stop until you achieve that target, but also don't spend all your profits because it will stop you re-investing and that will stop you hitting your target.

You have to keep coming back to your target to ensure you're reinvesting those profits until you achieve it, otherwise it is all too easy to start using those profits to fund your lifestyle and then you won't have the means available to keep pursuing new investments to bring you closer to that goal. If you reach a point where you're relying on that extra income to fund your lifestyle instead of investing it towards your target, then you've gone off course.

My mum, for example, cashed in a pension with the sole aim of investing it into property. When she got the cash, she booked a holiday. There's nothing wrong with that, but that's where it starts. I got a call from her saying, "Can I put the money in your letting agent's client account? Because I'm going to spend it." My mum is a superwoman – super intelligent, super ambitious, motivated and driven. She's my hero. I'm telling you that because even the best people in the world have the same temptations with cash.

It doesn't matter who you are – when you get cash, you also get the temptation to spend it. That's why I'm so insistent about setting a target and sticking to it. Don't spend your profits, use them to make more profits. When you reach your target, then you can spend your profits. If you've always been the type of person who spends money when you've got it, you should set a better system/process in place to make sure you're not spending it. It's not yours, it belongs to your plan.

My motivation is my kids. Every single penny my property investments generate is my kids' money and that makes it harder for me to spend it on anything that takes me off track from my target. Don't get me wrong, I'd love to have holidays and loads of cool stuff but, for now, my properties are part of a long-term plan for my kids and I am not going to waste the opportunity I'm creating for them just to have an extra holiday.

> **Top tip #6: Set yourself a goal and keep investing until you hit it. Don't stop.**

EVERYTHING EVENS OUT

The amount of profit you make from your property investments can and will fluctuate. One month you might make £500 from a particular property, the next it's down to £400 because of a repair you've had to pay for. Investors who get emotional will often get annoyed and fixate on that cost. They'll try to haggle or negotiate with contractors to drive the cost down and will either get frustrated that they can't or they'll try to cut corners. The worst part is that most landlords who fall into this trap don't even realise. Most landlords will see it as trying to save money or disputing some costs they've incurred.

You have to remember that you're playing the long game and that these kinds of expenses are unavoidable and will even out over the road to your long-term target. Instead you have to focus on what is within your control – such as rental rates and your mortgage repayments – and adjust those as and when you can and need to. On the flip side, you have to accept what you can't control, such as maintenance and repairs. Some months you'll make more, some months you'll make less. Over a year, you're trying to make a profit. Over 25 years you're trying to make a fortune.

The key is to treat the maintenance and repair costs as business expenses. Don't think of them as money you've "lost", instead consider them a normal cost of doing business in the world of property. It's a subtle but very important mindset that all anonymous landlords share.

People can get very stressed about those things they can't control, but remember that property is like any other investment. If you invested your money in Apple shares and expected a steady £500 a month profit you'd be disappointed. Investing doesn't work like that. What matters is the profit you finish with at the end of the year.

This is even more so with property. You don't just buy a property with a guarantee of £500 per month profit. Property investing requires you to continually invest, repair and improve. That's why property investment can be so profitable. It provides you with a monthly cash flow *and* it grows in value. But that's not free money. You have to continually invest to make sure your property investment is maintaining a good standard of compliance, a good standard for the tenant, and is secure in itself.

That's not to say that you shouldn't keep an eye on your profit month-to-month – because you need to make adjustments as you go – but simply be aware of what's in your control and what's not, and take a longer-term view than just one month at a time.

I've had to "fire" landlords from my lettings business because they cut corners and failed compliance purely because they'd become so heavily dependent on the income that they could not afford even the most simple and common of property repairs, even though they're required by law to repair those faults. I've seen landlords cut corners in the smallest ways and ended up with £30,000 fines! It's a serious business and cutting corners does not work. You might save £20 on a repair this month but you'll definitely lose a lot more than that in the long run.

THERE'S NO VALUE IN CUTTING CORNERS

Dave's tenant reported a rat problem. We sent the pest controller to the property who produced a report (as normal). The report advised that this property needed a specific type of trap to be installed in the ceiling, because there was a flat roof and the rats were living in the small roof space between. It was going to cost a couple of hundred pounds.

Dave decided not to take the advised action. The problem got worse, the tenant got more and more angry. We sent the pest controller to see if there was another solution. There wasn't. Dave was reluctant to spend the money, insisting it could be fixed just by filling in some holes in the wall with Polyfilla. The pest controller said this was a terrible idea; but nope, Dave got a builder out to fill in the holes.

A couple of weeks later, more rat problems – of course, those crafty creatures had found a new way into the kitchen! This time, the tenant reported it to the council. Guess what happened next?! I let Dave go too. It might seem like I get rid of bad customers a lot, but what's the point in paying a lettings management firm to manage your property if you're going to do it yourself anyway? Dave is one of the most stressed, time-poor, needy landlords we've come across and has constantly bounced from letting agent to letting agent.

TOP TIP #7: Play the long game. Sometimes you'll make a profit, sometimes you won't.

LETTING AGENTS AREN'T TRYING TO RIP YOU OFF

A lot of DIY and managed landlords think letting agents are trying to rip them off. I accept there are some rogue letting agents out there, some really crap agents; however, these idiots represent about five per cent of the industry. The rest of the letting agents are decent people that want to run a good business.

Nobody starts a letting agency to try and rip people off. However, so many people still believe that letting agents are out to steal their money. This could be because they've been charged £100 for a call out, for example. Just think about this logically. If your letting agent was going to commit fraud, they would need to include the tenant, their contractor and their staff. Everyone would have to be involved. Would they go to all that effort for just £100? £200? £500? No.

If someone is going to go to these lengths to rip you off, it's going to be for a lot more than £100. Also, you have to think logically about the person that you fear is going to rip you off. In most decent letting agents, there is a person or a team that handles property maintenance and repairs. They will not get your money. If they charge you for a repair, they don't see the money themselves.

I also understand the fear of letting someone else control your money. Especially if you're a traditional landlord who's used to collecting your rent and managing your own properties and tenancies. Once again, I come back to viewing property as any other investment. If you have shares in Apple and one month you receive a £500 dividend but the next month you only get £400, your immediate thought isn't going to be "Apple are ripping me off and trying to stitch me up." You know that's not how it works.

Apply that same logic to your property investments and, as I said in my previous point, treat a call-out fee as a normal business expense and remember that when you pay that £100, you're saving yourself the time, energy and mental stress of dealing with whatever issue has arisen.

Also, a good letting agent will have invested in software and systems which let you see all the transactions and expenses in real time – exactly the same way your online banking does. So really, there's not a lot of difference nowadays. You can see all activity at all times so it's near impossible for an agent to rip you off.

Lastly, if you are really unsure about an agent, remember that you can run this yourself. You can be an anonymous landlord by setting up your own team. The important thing is that you, your property and your tenancy are ALWAYS compliant, always maintained, always profitable and never taking up your time, energy, mind and family.

"Treat property like any other investment and detach yourself from it emotionally, rather than thinking of it as your home."

ANONYMOUS LANDLORD ACTION POINT

Do the maths for your next property deal and, if you're considering making a cash purchase, run the figures for buying with a buy-to-let mortgage so that you can compare the two. Come back to the target you set as part of your TOM – which of these options will get you closer to your target more quickly?

PART 3:

SETTING IT UP TO RUN AND GROW WITHOUT YOU

This final part of the book will help you get into the mindset of the anonymous landlord – remember this is all about thinking like a CEO and focusing on building a business rather than you being the business itself.

This might sound a bit too "high level" for some people but I promise you, this is the perfect mindset whether you have one property or 100 properties. It's simple too. The only reason it sounds complicated is because a lot of landlords would not consider themselves to be CEOs. I'm not going to turn you into a CEO, I'm going to give you some basic ways to implement the most fundamental elements of the CEO mindset with your properties. The most crucial aspect of this mindset is always asking, "Who can do this for me?"

I can't stress enough the importance of having a strong team to support you on your journey towards becoming an anonymous landlord, and it's *finding the who to help* that we'll start with in Chapter 7. Of course, finding the right people is just the beginning, once you have them in place you need to set up a system to allow them to work collaboratively and without requiring your guidance every step of the way. In a nutshell, this means setting this up in a way that allows your property business (and it *is* a business) to work and grow without you. Communication is key, and this is what we'll cover in Chapter 8.

Finally, in Chapter 9 I'll be sharing a blueprint for you to help you on your way to becoming an anonymous landlord. In fact, I'll share two blueprints, one of which will guide you if you have yet to invest in property, and the other will help you build your property investing business if you are already a landlord.

In both instances, the key is having the right mindset and thinking like a property investor rather than like a landlord. Building any business relies on having a team to support you. You might not think of yourself as a business owner – that's OK. I'm here to tell you that you already are. It's not complicated, so let's start with how and where you can find the who to help.

7 FINDING THE WHO TO HELP

Alex stands back, hands on hips, feeling pretty proud. At his feet is a roller tray with the dregs of paint in it and a rather well-used roller, ready to be cleaned. "Almost there!" He thinks as he begins to tidy up.

The following weekend Alex is surveying his handiwork while waiting for his IKEA delivery to arrive. He checks his phone for what feels like the millionth time, noting that he still has 45 minutes of his two-hour delivery window to wait. He looks out of the window onto the street and feels a wave of relief as he spots a delivery van heading his way. Half an hour later, he's surrounded by boxes and is wondering where to start when there's a knock at the door.

"Come in, it's open," he yells, turning to see Jenny walk through the door. "When you said you needed a hand putting together a couple of bits of furniture, I didn't think you meant you'd bought everything in IKEA," she says with a grin. Alex sheepishly smiles back, "I know, it's a lot, but I'm sure it won't take long with the two of us ..." Jenny laughs, "You owe me dinner for this!"

Several hours later, Jenny is collapsed on the newly assembled sofa, cup of tea in hand. "Jen, can you just hop off the sofa for a sec, I'm going to take some photos for the advert."

"What, now?"

"Yeah, thought I might as well while I'm here, save a trip tomorrow."

"But the light has gone – really you want to photograph this room in the morning, it'll look a lot nicer." Alex frowns, "Hmmm, you're probably right, guess I'll be back tomorrow."

"Can't the letting agent come and do the photos?"

"Well, they could if I was using one ..." Alex replies, "I figured I could list it on Facebook myself, it's not that hard to take a few photos and write a property description." Now it's Jenny's turn to frown. "Suit yourself, would have thought you'd save yourself the hassle though."

Two weeks later, Alex is remembering Jenny's words. He's been to the house three times already this week to show prospective tenants around and he's got 15 more enquiries in his inbox, although he liked the second couple he met. He reaches for his phone. "Darren? Hi, it's Alex Banks, from the house on Cranleigh Road?"

"Hi Alex, great to hear from you, did you need something else from us?"

"Actually I wanted to offer you the house, assuming you're still interested?"

"Amazing! Yes please, we'd love to accept."

"Fantastic, I'll get the paperwork over to you this evening and then we can go from there." Alex smiles as he hangs up, he's definitely getting there.

An hour later, as he's cooking dinner, Alex has a nagging feeling he's forgotten something. Earlier he'd felt so elated knowing that Darren and his partner would be moving in, but he can't shake a slight sinking feeling in his stomach – then it hits him! He hasn't asked Darren for any references. He lets out an audible sigh – he's already sent the paperwork. Can he ask for them now? Take it back? Alex doesn't know if he's even able to do that.

He takes a couple of deep breaths. They are nice people. "Stop stressing Alex, it'll all be fine. You're worrying over nothing," he tells himself. Only, he can't quite silence the voice asking, "But will it?"

Finding the who to help you is one of the most important steps on your journey to becoming an anonymous landlord. One of the big challenges is often that a lot of the jobs you need to delegate in order to become an anonymous landlord are tasks that you're capable of doing yourself. It can be really tempting to think you'll "just" do things yourself – but do you want to end up like Alex, having to deal with every step yourself?

I'm a businessman and, before I got into the habit of thinking like a businessman, I would say things like "I'll just get this done myself", or "leave it with me", or "it's quicker if I just do this myself." It's the illusion of saving money and time because all these tasks were within my capabilities. However, this took up my time, energy, mind, and took me away from my family. Just to try and save some money.

But this can be a genuine challenge, because each of the tasks you need to complete to rent out a property can feel small on their own, and in many cases simple. However, when you put them all together they can add up to a lot of work. Plus, when you make the decision to take responsibility for these things yourself, you are also committing to them at all times of day or night.

In many cases, the law requires you to take immediate action and follow specific procedures at all times of the day or night. If you invested in property in order to become a tenancy manager, property manager or administrator then I take all this back and wish you all the best. However, I'm pretty sure, if you're reading a book called *The Anonymous Landlord* then you didn't.

Another way to think of it is as though you're a chef. Now, if you're the chef you're going to add ingredients to your pan and maybe give them a stir with a spoon, but you're not going to get into the pan with the ingredients. If you invest in a restaurant business, you're probably going to employ a chef to cook the food, and a waiter to serve the food. Even though you could probably whip up some soup or a pizza yourself, that's not why you invested in a restaurant and it's not what you specialise in.

It's the same when you're an anonymous landlord – you're overseeing what goes into your "pan" but at no point are you jumping in yourself. You're putting the right people in the right place to do the job correctly.

Many people think that when they do everything themselves, they're saving money, but that is very rarely the case. First, you have to think about what your time is worth. If you could earn £50 an hour, then every hour you spend doing those little jobs that you could delegate costs you £50, not to mention detracting from your other pots of profit. If you're a parent, it's just another reason to take a phone call. Your kids don't know what you're doing, they just see one more thing that's more important than them.

Then there's the rent. Most DIY landlords don't charge the full market value rent because they are scared of losing a good tenant. That's like giving money away. Most landlords in this position will avoid that conversation so they end up justifying to themselves why they don't need to bring the rent up to a fair market value. But if I asked you for £50 a month for no reason, you would tell me to p*ss off. Don't get me started on the amount landlords are being fined now for being non-compliant. Did you know, most landlords are either non-compliant or in "poor practice" and they don't even know it? That's scary now with £30,000 fines being imposed and councils setting up task forces to go and get that money.

The other way to look at it is from the perspective of what you'd look for if you were to hire someone to do the task for you. Let's say you're looking for someone to help you find a tenant for your property. You have two options: someone inexperienced who's never done this before and who is charging £250; or someone with lots of experience, good connections and a strong track record who is charging £500. You would probably pick the person with experience who's charging £500 right? I would hope so.

However, when you choose to do this yourself, you're effectively choosing the inexperienced person who doesn't have the best possible resources available. You might be saving yourself £500, but are you going to do the best job (be honest with yourself)?

What's more, you're not really saving yourself the full amount of money because you're investing your time, energy, mind and spending less time with your family. If you're able to earn £50 per hour doing something you're expert at, you should pay someone else to fix the house while you go and earn £50 per hour! Then the house repairs pay for themselves.

The hardest part of this process of finding people to help you as you become an anonymous landlord is learning to let go. I tell the landlords I work with that "You've got to let it go to let it grow," but I know accepting that someone else will do those jobs for you can be difficult. This is all part of the mindset shift you need to make to become an anonymous landlord, though.

There are five steps you need to take as part of this letting go process:

1. Ask, **"WHO CAN DO THESE THINGS FOR ME?"** Another way to approach this question is to think about who you would find to do those tasks if you physically couldn't do them yourself.

2. Next, you need to **PUT THOSE PEOPLE IN PLACE**.

3. Once you have the right people, you need to **SET EXPECTATIONS** with each of them.

4. You then need to set up a system that allows you to **MANAGE AND MONITOR** those people to ensure they're achieving the expectations you've set.

5. Finally, it's essential that you **TREAT THE PEOPLE SUPPORTING YOU LIKE PARTNERS**.

FINDING THE WHO

There are very few things relating to property investment that you need to do yourself, which means the vast majority of tasks that you're currently involved with can be outsourced to other people. The only exception (and the only thing that I still do myself in my property business) is signing legal documents when you purchase a property.

Everything else can be outsourced – whether that's sourcing a property, the purchase process, processing the mortgage, refurbishing the property, advertising it and finding tenants, compliance, or the ongoing management of the property and the tenancy. In addition to the tasks related directly to your property investment, you also have activities related to your business and its administration – such as renewing mortgages, tax and accounting, legal processes, insurances.

One of my top pieces of advice is to make sure that everyone you work with, as a minimum, is a specialist in the field of property and property investing and, ideally, that they are active property investing landlords themselves. The reason I recommend you work with other property investors is that they have the creativity, knowledge and experience to solve problems, proactively reduce risk, and give you sound advice.

When you know something yourself, especially from experience, you know what warning signs to look out for. If you can find people for your team who have that knowledge and can spot potential problems, you'll find everything runs much more smoothly.

Personally, I only work with people and partners who are property investors and landlords themselves – my mortgage adviser, my solicitor, my accountant, my contractors, my sourcing agents. This has been invaluable for me.

If you already own one or more buy-to-let properties and aren't intending to grow your portfolio any further, you won't need the people related to finding and refurbishing a property. But let's look at where you can find the right people for every aspect of your property investment business, regardless of what your business looks like.

SOURCING A PROPERTY

You ideally want to find sourcing agents, property brokers and estate agents to work with you on finding a property. Generally speaking, I prefer to work with sourcing agents and property brokers because they are engaged by you as the buyer, and it's you who pays them. They are great at finding properties that are below market value, that are a good investment and/or offer an opportunity to increase the value.

When it comes to finding the best property deals, sourcing agents or property brokers are usually more reliable. The key to getting the most out of your relationship with a sourcing agent or property broker is to give them a very clear brief – set your expectations.

As well as telling them what type of property you're looking for (a three-bedroom house) and where (in Portsmouth), tell them how much you're prepared to spend on a refurbishment and what level of work you are comfortable with (i.e. you're happy to refurbish but you don't want a property that requires any structural or building work).

In addition, tell them how much you're willing to spend in cash, how you're financing your purchase (with a mortgage, usually) and whether you're happy to refinance and leave any money in the property once it's let.

Remember I said, "Don't chase unicorns, buy a workhorse"? This is music to a sourcing agent's ears. Imagine how many people they speak to who ask for a property that "they can get ALL their money back out from" or "will make them £30,000 profit" or "will generate 50 per cent ROI". Be realistic and logical with your expectations and a sourcing agent will work their socks off for you. If you ask for a unicorn, you won't get as much attention.

Providing your sourcing agent with a clear and detailed brief that covers all of those points will help ensure that the properties they bring you align with your investment strategy. I've always found the best sourcing agents and property brokers are ex-estate agents, because they do a really great job of managing the sale and know how to look after you as the buyer.

Beware, however, as there are lots of people who have done a sourcing course and then fancy themselves as sourcing agents. I've heard of sourcing agents who simply go to Rightmove, find any house and then tell remote investors it's "below market value" so they can charge you a sourcing fee. Unfortunately, there are rogue sourcing agents, so watch out for them. It's the same in most industries but you always have to watch out for the idiots. One way to spot a good sourcing agent is to speak to their clients, or check their qualifications, accreditations, and experience.

It is also useful to build relationships with estate agents, because they may bring properties to you when something suitable comes onto the market. However, always remember that the estate agent gets paid by (and therefore is working for) the seller. Ideally you want an estate agent who will bring you properties before they go on the open market. You should always trust your own due diligence too.

I use sourcing agents to find all of my property investments because, in my experience, they tend to find the best investment deals and are more likely to find properties that are for sale at below their market value. Using sourcing agents and property brokers is how you become an anonymous landlord, because they not only find the properties, but also carry out due diligence based on your instructions. Personally, I quite enjoy doing the due diligence so I have the sourcing agents bring me the information. That's how I'm an anonymous landlord in this part of the process. I have two options:

1. I find all the information myself

2. I ask, "Who can get this information for me?"

While estate agents might bring you some good deals, it will then be down to you to check the properties and carry out your own due diligence. So, building relationships with estate agents can be useful but is more of a DIY approach to property investment. If you really enjoy the process of finding and viewing properties, negotiating on price and getting the deal, by all means use estate agents. To really find the right property deals, you might need to view 20 properties, make ten offers and hope to get one accepted. Or, you can pay a sourcing agent to do that because that's what they do.

As I've said before, the point of becoming an anonymous landlord is to remove you from the aspects of being a landlord that are onerous, you don't need to do and that you don't enjoy, so if there are parts of this process that you love getting involved in, then by all means continue, just know that there are people who can provide support in this area too.

TOP TIPS FOR FINDING THE RIGHT SOURCING AGENT OR PROPERTY BROKER

When you're looking for a sourcing agent or property broker, it's important that you check they have the right insurance as well as the relevant accreditations – this may vary depending on the type of sourcing agent or property broker you're looking for, but typically includes professional indemnity insurance, registration with the Information Commissioner's Office, anti-money laundering registration with HMRC, and membership with a redress or property ombudsman scheme.

Ideally, they will also have an estate agency or decent property background; they'll be willing to let you talk to previous clients and they'll have a good understanding of all parts of property investing and landlording. In my experience, a great sourcing agent is an investor themselves and an ex-estate agent.

Beyond this, it can be difficult to tell a "good" sourcing agent or property broker from a "bad" one until you start working with them and, really, the proof is in the results they provide.

When you start working with an agent or a broker, you need to do your own due diligence – this is essential. However, the benefit you have when it comes to finding a sourcing agent or property broker is that they give you their "product" before you pay them anything, because their fee will only be payable if you decide to buy the property they bring to you.

So, when a sourcing agent or property broker brings you a property you need to do your own due diligence to check whether they have understood your brief and done a thorough job of meeting it. Let's say a new sourcing agent brings me a three-bedroom house. One of the first things I'll do is take the property details and check it against current property values.

If that sourcing agent is good, the property they've found for me will be a good deal below current market value. However, if the sourcing agent is bringing me a three-bedroom property for £100,000 but my research shows that similar properties are selling for £90,000 in the same area, I can immediately see that they haven't done a very good job. This would probably be the last time I talk to that sourcing agent unless there's a good reason for this error.

Once you've been working with a sourcing agent or property broker for a number of years, and built a strong relationship, you may trust that their research is good and therefore you'll decide you don't need to carry out your own due diligence any longer or you just check over the information they provide. This is the point I've reached with my sourcing agents.

PURCHASING A PROPERTY

Working with the right solicitor is essential when you're buying invest-ment properties, because they are the professionals who make sure that everything to do with the property is above board from a legal perspective, and that you're protected in your purchase. They gather information from various sources, including the local council and the seller's solicitor, and make sure that there are no red flags for the property in question, whether that's relating to a road being built through the middle of the house in a few years' time, restrictions on drainage or making sure the plot you're buying is legally able to be sold.

A good solicitor is worth their weight in gold, because they will make sure that you're not unduly restricted with the property you're buying and that there are no significant issues that could affect the safety or value of that property in the future.

For example, a solicitor will pick up on whether a property is located in an area that's a flood risk and would then make sure that the appropri-ate surveys are carried out, that the council isn't planning to demolish the property because of its flood risk, and that you can get insurance for your property to cover flooding. Your solicitor will put relevant indemnities in place to protect you where there is uncertainty or a lack of information. They will also tell you whether the property has any restrictive covenants on it, or whether it's a listed building or located in a protected area.

This is important to know when you come to make changes or refurbish the property, because if a property is listed or in a protected area, you may be limited on the changes you are allowed to make to it. Knowing this before you go ahead with your purchase allows you to make an informed decision about whether it's still the right property for you.

TOP TIPS FOR FINDING THE RIGHT SOLICITOR

If you're buying your property through an estate agent, my top tip is to use the estate agent's solicitor for the purchase, provided they are a local solicitor (rather than one who's part of a national legal firm).

This is my personal preference. I've worked in estate agency for a number of years and I also own a property sales agency now. In that time, I've worked with national law firms, local law firms and online law firms. In 90 per cent of those cases, the local law firms have been the best, by far. So, if a local estate agent recommends a local law firm, that's because they are reliable.

The reasons for this are – firstly, that a local solicitor who is already working with that estate agency will have a relationship with the agent, which can make the whole process smoother. Secondly, it's fair to assume that the solicitor the estate agent uses (and recommends to sellers) will be good, because it's in the agent's interest to get property sales to go through as they only get paid on completion of a sale. Therefore, a local estate agent will rarely choose to work with an ineffective law firm because they are less likely to get paid.

In fact, the majority of complaints that estate agents face come during the time when the solicitor is supposed to be doing their job of getting the sale to exchange and then complete. It therefore isn't in the estate agent's interests to recommend a rubbish or inefficient solicitor to their sellers.

The other way to find a good solicitor is to look at how much they charge for their conveyancing services. Generally, cheaper does not equal better. In fact, in almost all instances, cheaper means a worse service. If a solicitor is competing on cost and undercutting other solicitors in their area, I would take that as a sign that they're not very good at their job and therefore don't have many (or any) repeat clients.

Secondly, if a solicitor is charging considerably less than their competitors, it likely means they aren't paying as many staff and that can mean that the conveyancing process takes longer because each solicitor in their practice has a higher case load. There isn't a way to shortcut the conveyancing process – there are set steps that every solicitor has to go through, so fewer employees just means that process will take a bit longer.

In my experience of investing in property and being in property for over 20 years, the cheap solicitors are always the worst and are a false economy.

It is also advisable to look for a solicitor who specialises in property investing and development, especially if you are looking to build a long-term relationship with a single firm of solicitors who can help you with all your future property purchases.

Remember my tip about trying to work with people and partners who are investors, landlords or experienced in property investing. For example, 80 per cent of my personal solicitor's business is property, development, investment and conveyancing. For me, that makes them specialists – certainly more so than a regular solicitor.

My final tip, which doesn't just apply to finding a solicitor, is that you should never haggle over the price of services. Haggle over the price of physical products, by all means, but when it comes to paying for a service, just go with the price they set out. Why? If a company or person is providing you with a service, you want them to provide you with the best service possible.

If you've haggled and squeezed all the juice out of that agreement so that you make more money and the service provider makes less, it's more likely you won't get the full service. It's more likely that the service provider will not be as motivated to go above and beyond for you. It's more likely that the service provider will not work as hard for you or put as much effort into you. You do not want that, as the recipient of the service. So do not haggle services, haggle products.

FINANCING A PROPERTY

I talked extensively about the different ways to finance a property purchase in Chapter 6 and the professional you will need to support you in this area is a mortgage broker. As I explained in the last chapter, they can help you find the best deals for financing your property purchases.

TOP TIPS FOR FINDING THE RIGHT MORTGAGE BROKER

Similar to solicitors, if you can find a mortgage broker who specialises in property investing, you'll be in a much stronger position because they will have in-depth knowledge of buy-to-let mortgages, bridging loans and development finance, among other things, that a general mortgage broker will likely be lacking.

Not all mortgage brokers will advertise themselves as specialists in property investment finance, however, so it always pays to ask that question when you get in touch with a mortgage broker.

It can also be really helpful if your mortgage broker is a landlord or property investor themselves, because that means they understand both sides of the fence and will have a good grasp of your objectives. My mortgage broker, for example, is an investor and a landlord. In fact, he's an anonymous landlord which fills me with pride. It means he has a broader perspective on property because he's highly experienced in the actual mortgage side as well as the investing side.

Finally, I'll reiterate the "cheaper is worse" rule. When it comes to mortgage brokers, a decent one will get paid a broker fee by the borrower (that's you in this scenario) as well as a commission by the lender when they set up a mortgage.

Now, there are some mortgage brokers who offer no fees for you, the client. That might sound great but in my experience these mortgage brokers never do a very good job. I imagine that's because there just isn't enough money in the transaction, so they operate on economies of scale and that means they'll be trying to arrange a lot of mortgages quickly so you won't necessarily get the same level of service you will from someone who charges a fee.

It's the same in most service industries. Some companies aim for low income from high volume. Other companies aim for high income from lower volume. The best companies are the combination of the two. The ones that charge a high enough fee to be able to put maximum time and effort into each and every customer while maintaining a healthy profit – those are the best.

While you might not want to pay a company to help them make profit, you really do want every partner you work with to be profitable themselves. If a company is profitable, it means they're reliable for you, they have money to invest in the development of their staff, systems and processes, training and quality of service. That sounds really cheesy, but it means that you must only work with profitable companies so that you know there is minimal risk of them going bust, or being tempted to cut corners.

REFURBISHING A PROPERTY

I'm not going to list all the tradespeople you'll need for property refurbishment; instead my advice is to find a reliable building firm that covers all trades. In doing so, I know that they will manage the entire project and bring in whoever is needed for a given job, whether that's a plumber, an electrician, a carpenter or a decorator. Additionally, a decent building firm will have vetted and checked their tradespeople, and they'll have the right insurance, qualifications, accreditations and facilities.

A great way to find really good contractors is to speak to a local letting agent. Inevitably, the letting agent will work with reliable contractors because they need to rely on them in a lot of cases to carry out maintenance and repairs. The chances are, the letting agent will have built a very good relationship with good contractors because it's almost an extension of their business. So, ask a local letting agent for an intro to a good contractor.

Another good option is to speak to your sourcing agent or property broker about whether they would also be prepared to project manage the refurbishment – in many cases they are happy to also act as your project manager and, again, that means you don't have to find all the tradespeople for the project.

Remember that building contractors will often be prepared to do more than just carry out the refurbishment work. For instance, if you are fitting a new kitchen you can ask your kitchen fitter or project manager to source all of the white goods as part of the job. Don't get me wrong, they will charge you for doing this, but better that you pay a little extra than you have to spend the time finding and buying all of those appliances.

Similarly, I trust my contractors to make design decisions about the kitchens or bathrooms they're fitting. They are usually aware of the latest trends in home decor and I know they'll make sound decisions. It's another way in which I can take a step back, and it's this that enables me to be an anonymous landlord.

This is also the stage at which I would bring in a letting agent, because if they are good then they will be prepared to go to the property and advise your contractors to ensure that all the work they're doing is compliant with regulations around rental properties and that it will appeal to the market you're targeting for your property.

Overall, you should bring in the right people to manage the full project because that's what they're good at.

MANAGING THE PROPERTY AND FINDING TENANTS

Once your property is ready to let, the next step is finding tenants. When you're meeting tenants and "vetting" them yourself, it can be easy to fall into the trap of offering your property to a tenant who seems like a nice person without carrying out the proper checks or, worse, ignoring certain information because you got a good feeling about them.

However, you have to remember that an interview for renting a property is like a job interview – the person you're interviewing is acting in a certain way to get their desired result. Everyone does that in an interview! That doesn't mean every nice person you meet is pretending, but you can't rely on your impressions from the interview alone.

It can also be easy to accept tenants who are far from ideal because you feel as though you need to just get someone into your property. That means you might miss some important facts or cut a few corners to get a tenant in place.

APPEARANCES CAN BE DECEIVING

Back in the days when I was doing everything in my lettings business, I remember taking a charming single mum of two for a viewing at a property. Sally was very pleasant and seemed really nice. We hadn't had much interest in this property, so when she asked for a second viewing the landlord, George, came along to meet her as well. He had the same impression – a personable, pleasant lady. George wanted her to move in.

I could easily have been blinded by her personality, taken the landlord's instruction and moved her in; but I stuck to the process and carried out referencing and vetting as normal. Through my investigations, I discovered Sally had CCJs, was evicted from her previous property and that her income was made up of benefits and some part-time work.

Now, having benefits as an income isn't an issue. However, the council can withdraw someone's benefits without any warning if they suspect they are making any additional income – even if that's only £5 a week! As a result, it's common for tenants who are on benefits to have a guarantor – someone who will guarantee the rent if the tenant doesn't pay. Personally I insist on guarantors wherever I can (it's the investor in me, protecting against risk), but you can't always get guarantors.

A bit of further digging revealed that Sally had moved out of her last property because of "problems with her previous neighbours", but she had always paid the rent without issue. I presented all of this information to George, as my lettings management company was only finding a tenant, we weren't managing the property because he wanted to save money.

The property had been empty for two months and George was getting desperate, so he moved Sally in. A few months later, my lettings management company got a call from a neighbour, complaining about Sally having late night parties, aggressive shouting and screaming, and a constant smell of weed – all of which we reported to George.

Some time later, George called asking for advice. Sally had stopped paying rent because her benefits had been withdrawn as she was working more hours than she'd declared. It turned out that the problems she'd had with her previous neighbours were exactly what had been reported to us. It took George eight months to evict her, during which time he received no rent, AND she caused £3,000 of damage to the property. Lovely.

Ultimately she was a terrible tenant but a very good actor!

I could share dozens of stories just like this one (and plenty worse! I know of one tenant who turned the property they were renting into a drug den and, just like Sally in that example, she had come across as a very pleasant person at the viewing). When you take control of the process of finding tenants yourself, you run the risk of cutting corners or being taken in by someone who is a very good actor.

This is just one reason why finding a letting agency to manage your property (or properties) is a good idea. They will have a process for vetting and investigating potential tenants so, at the very least, you go into it with your eyes open and, at best, you avoid letting your property to a bad tenant in the first place.

TOP TIPS FOR FINDING THE RIGHT LETTING AGENT

Most letting agents will tell you that they are "different" or "better" than other agents in your area, but the key question to ask them is, "How are you different/better?" It's not enough for agents to market themselves as providing "good customer service" – every business should do that! What you are looking for are facts that prove a letting agent is set up to provide a reliable, robust, secure service to both landlords and tenants.

Some of the tangible factors to ask about include: an automated payment system; a local point of contact; emergency services and systems in place for tenants *and* landlords 24/7; advice and support services in all areas of the

---

property industry; whether the owner of the agency is an investor landlord themselves; connections to professionals like mortgage brokers, refurbishment contractors and project managers; and the accreditations, qualifications and ongoing education of their staff.

You should be looking for a letting agent who is confident and assertive with tenants and with you. You want a letting agent who will take charge instead of taking orders, which means they will tell you what's required to make sure you're profitable, compliant, legal and secure; and that they will deal with immediate issues promptly, informing you about the problem and the solution – rather than coming to you with a problem and waiting for you to provide the solution.

How a letting agent communicates is also important. You should find out whether they have multiple means of communication, which can range from email and phone to WhatsApp groups, text messaging and even online platforms that you can log into to see details about your properties and their management.

Also, ask letting agents about their processes and departmental structure – do they have dedicated departments for finance, maintenance and tenant management, or does everyone do everything? You are ideally looking for an agent that has specialist departments and robust processes that everyone follows.

You also want a letting agent who will protect your investment, by which I mean they will ensure you are always charging rent that is in-line with market values and that you aren't spending more money than you need to on the maintenance of your properties.

Ultimately, you are looking for a letting agent who sells their services using facts, rather than emotional selling points that they can't possibly prove (no agent can categorically state they work harder or care more than any other agent out there!). A good letting agent will also be honest about not being cheap – you're not looking for cheap! You're looking for good value, and a good letting agent will be able to tell you what value they can deliver for you.

The big deciding factor is the people working within a letting agency, because this truly is what differentiates one from another. Now, I'm not saying you should just choose the agent you like over one that has all the processes and systems in place (a robust and well-run letting agent wins every time!) but if there's not much between them, then of course the people matter.

I'd also add that I believe the best letting agents are owned by investor landlords – or, better yet, anonymous landlords – because that means they've set up the entire business to focus on managing properties successfully and automatically.

YOU GET WHAT YOU PAY FOR

Whether you're looking for a sourcing agent, a solicitor, a building contractor, letting agent or a mortgage broker, the old adage, "You get what you pay for" holds true. Ultimately, the less you pay your mortgage broker or solicitor, the more you will have to do yourself – which is the opposite of what you want if you're aiming to become an anonymous landlord.

For example, my mortgage broker fills in my mortgage application forms for me, because he already has the majority of the information he needs. That means he doesn't need to send me lots of forms to fill in when he's approaching different lenders to arrange a mortgage on my behalf. It's the same with my solicitor, who will make decisions on my behalf that are in my best interests. He'll arrange the mortgage valuations for me, follow them up, argue them (if needed), and chase up every party involved in the whole transaction. How great is that!?!?

My solicitor will make recommendations *after* they have collected the right information, rather than coming to me and asking if I'd like them to look into something (which, if they've identified it as a potential issue, I absolutely will). In some cases, my solicitor will liaise directly with my mortgage broker to get the information they need about the lender I'm using, again taking me out of the process. I might pay a bit more for their services as a result, but as far as I'm concerned that's money well spent to save my time and energy.

For example, I've pre-instructed my solicitor to take the necessary indemnities out if required or if it's the best thing to do. They don't need to ask me for permission on every single detail, they are the best people to know exactly what to do in every instance. I'm not legally trained, I don't know what is the best course of action. Your solicitor just needs the authorisation to act on your behalf.

Similarly, my sourcing agent will provide me with a refurb estimate on any property they present me with. I usually get my contractor to view the property with the sourcing agent and provide me with their refurb estimate as well – in many cases this will broadly match up and, if you've allowed additional funds for a contingency as I've recommended then, as long as the estimates aren't wildly different, you should still be okay.

HOW THE PROCESS WORKS IN PRACTICE

When you have the right people in all of these positions, you will discover that the process of finding, buying, refurbishing and letting a property becomes a well-oiled machine. This is how it typically works in my property business ...

A sourcing agent will bring me a property and I'll check their due diligence. In some cases, I may not even need to do that depending on the property, its location and the agent in question. If the sourcing agent says the property needs a refurb, I'll send my contractor to have a look and provide me with an estimate for the work. In most cases, they'll do this free of charge because they know the work will come to them. Once all of that is confirmed, I go ahead with the purchase and my solicitor and mortgage broker take it from there. In other cases, the sourcing agent will already be in contact with my contractors and the information the agent provides is confirmed.

When we are going to exchange contracts, or we're a week away from completion, I'll let my contractor know. They will then arrange to collect the keys from the selling agent, which allows them to start work straight away. My letting agent will coordinate with my building contractor to ensure all the work is done properly and to the right standards. This also means that my letting agent is already in the loop, so as soon as the property is ready they can get it on the market, ensuring I get tenants in place as quickly as possible.

My letting agent then takes on management of every part of the entire process. I give them the freedom of "if it's got to be done, get it done". I don't need to know about every repair or compliance job that's needed at the property. What will I do with that information?

This is the benefit of having a team of the right people around you, because it takes a lot of the work away from you and ensures that everything is done efficiently, compliantly and to a high standard.

I know landlords who insist on being asked permission for every single job. Why? If the letting agent says to you, "Would you like us to carry out this repair which is legally required for you to be a compliant landlord?" What are you going to say? Yes, obviously. So why waste everyone's time? Give your agent the go ahead in advance. If it can be deducted from the rent and it's got to be done, get it done.

Remember, "You've got to let it go to let it grow."

ANONYMOUS LANDLORD ACTION POINT

Make a list of all the jobs related to your property (or properties) that you currently do yourself. Go through that list and highlight all of the ones you could easily outsource. Choose just one of those, research local professionals in that area and find the right person to take it off your list. All gone well? Work through your list and remember, sometimes one person can take multiple tasks away from you. It's all about finding the right *who*.

8 SETTING UP THE FLOW OF COMMUNICATION

THE LIFE OF AN ANONYMOUS LANDLORD

When I sit down at my computer and I see an email from my sourcing agent who has found me a new potential property, I break into a smile – this is one of my favourite parts of property investing. I love calculating, producing strategies and getting stuck into the creative side of property. One of the only jobs I keep (and only because I genuinely enjoy it) is doing the due diligence on the properties I'm considering buying.

Back to my emails. As usual, my sourcing agent has neatly laid out all the pertinent information: the valuation of the property, comparisons with other sold properties in the area, rent value and estimated refurbishment costs.

All my sourcing agents and property brokers know that, when they send me a property, I want the investment opportunity to be supported by objective information. I've set clear expectations about what I'm looking for from them and, by and large, they always deliver. It doesn't take too much of my time to see that this property looks like a good choice.

I ping an email to my mortgage adviser, copying in both the sourcing agent and my solicitor. I know that they'll sort everything out between them from here. They copy me into their communications, and I love seeing their exchanges, particularly when my mortgage adviser quizzes the agent on certain aspects of the property or challenges them. I know he's got my best interests at heart and I know that once everything is sorted, the relevant paperwork will come my way for a signature. Until then, I just sit back and watch.

My mortgage adviser and I have been working together for years, so he fills in and submits the mortgage applications on my behalf, only coming to me if there's something tricky I need to be aware of, or to let me know if he thinks I should walk away from a particular property.

In the meantime, I've seen emails from my solicitor going back and forth with both the agent and my mortgage adviser. My solicitor contacts me directly once we have a rough completion date in place. It's time for me to make another connection, this time putting my contractors in touch with the selling agent and authorising them to collect the keys on the day of completion.

I also tell my contractor my budget for the refurbishment, the end value I'm aiming for, and that I want to rent this property out. As we've worked with this particular agent before, they let my contractor visit the property ahead of completion, so by the time they're collecting the keys I already have an estimate for the works and have agreed to it – as always my contractor has come in at the budget I set.

When completion day comes around, my contractor and their team get straight to work. They know I'm good for the money and they also know what I expect from a refurbishment that's going to be rented. I get the odd photo update and an offer to view the property, but I rarely bother these days – I've seen thousands of houses in my time and, in all honesty, if I'm not going to live there then I'm not too bothered.

That scenario isn't unusual in my life as an anonymous landlord – if you like the sound of this, then know that you too can have a property investment business that runs smoothly, like a well-oiled machine, with very little involvement from you.

Finding the right people to be part of your team is just one step on your journey towards becoming an anonymous landlord – albeit a very important step. The next stage is to make sure that they all communicate with one another – you want to avoid becoming a middleman, where you're just passing information between two of your specialists. There's no need for you to be in that position, so remove yourself from it and let your team get on with what they do best.

Your job is to connect people so that they can share information between themselves. Once you've made the right connections, everything just flows.

Personally, I get a real buzz from seeing the process happen without me. I find it incredibly rewarding to know that I've set this up, and with everyone communicating with one another effectively, I can just watch it all unfold, almost like a movie I've made playing out in front of my eyes. Perhaps more importantly, I know I'm building assets and wealth for my family without sacrificing my time, energy, mind or their time. What's the point in making profit from property if I'm sacrificing other things for it?

I have developed strong relationships with my mortgage adviser, solicitor, sourcing agents and contractors, which means that we all trust one another to do our jobs. My contractors, for example, know that they have autonomy to choose fixtures and fittings for a refurbishment project. I don't need to pick out the work surfaces or the carpet, they are more than capable of doing that on my behalf.

We also have an agreement where I pay their entire project fee on completion, but this wasn't always how we operated. When I first started out, I would pay 25 per cent up front, and then the remaining 75 per cent over three equal instalments. The 25 per cent up front should cover the cost of materials, allowing you to pay the rest as the job progresses. That progressed to me paying for materials in advance and the balance on completion. Sometimes I still do this.

All of my contractors also know there is a ten per cent contingency built into every project, so should plaster come off the walls when they're removing wallpaper, or they discover a couple of floorboards in the kitchen are rotten, they know there will be no problem covering those additional costs.

Bringing in a project manager can allow you to take a further step back, because they can liaise not only with the contractors, but also the letting agent to ensure that the property goes onto the market as soon as possible.

If I'm planning to refinance the property once the refurbishment is completed, all I need to do is let my mortgage adviser know that the work is finished, and forward them the details the contractor has provided me about the work they've undertaken. Then they can explore the financing options available and just send me the paperwork to sign once they've found the right deal.

STAY IN YOUR LANE

The key to having a team that works well together is that everyone knows what is expected of them and what their boundaries are, but also that everyone is able to take ownership of *their* lane. Your lane is as the owner of the business, the CEO who is making strategic decisions and nothing more. Stay there and allow the team of specialists you have carefully assembled to use their expertise and do their best work.

When you treat everyone like partners, set clear targets and allow them to achieve their objectives in their own way, they enjoy their work more, they do better work for you and you have a lot less to do. You don't have to micromanage because you have set very clear expectations.

Come back to TOM – you set the target for each of your specialists; they should then set out the objectives to achieve that target and they should also know the method to reach their objectives.

As a general rule of thumb, the best property investors I've ever met or worked with are the ones who stay in their lane. They don't try to get involved in every little detail, they just set sensible boundaries and allow everyone else to own and manage their lanes.

I now even have someone making and managing all the payments from my accounts. It's one less thing that I'm required for. After all, I didn't get into property investing so I could do all this myself. In fact, it's the exact opposite. I wanted to build wealth and assets so that I could stop working and spend time with my kids. That's it!

SETTING UP YOUR POWER TEAM

The following is an overview of all the professionals you'll need on your power team to enable you to become an anonymous landlord, as well as a brief overview of the expectations I've set with the people on my power team. Setting up your property business in this way is vital for your success.

MORTGAGE BROKER

- My adviser completes as much of the paperwork as possible. I do not want to complete forms and applications.

- I connect them with the selling agent, so if they need property information they can get it directly.

- I have a financial controller, so I connected them with my mortgage adviser, enabling them to request payments for things like surveyors, broker fees etc.

SOLICITOR

- Similarly, I don't want to fill out forms so I connect my solicitor with the selling agent and my mortgage broker to collect the information they need.

- I tell them to act for me in relation to things like indemnity policies – "If it's the best choice to get the purchase complete, get it done."

- At worst, all I have to do is go into the solicitor to sign papers when a purchase is ready to complete. However, during lockdown we started signing over Zoom and then sending paperwork in the post (guess who walked to the postbox? Not me).

LETTING AGENT
- Letting a property – I don't need to know all the offers from all the tenants. I tell the lettings team my top and bottom price and they can negotiate on my behalf. The more rent they achieve, the better their fee. Okay, so it's my letting agency, but 99 per cent of agents work on a percentage of rent so it's the same rule.

- I tell them – if it needs doing, get it done. If it's going to cost more than the rent, spread it over two payments if possible. If the contractor won't accept that, then you can request a payment from me, but only then.

ACCOUNTANT
- I think you see the pattern here. I don't want to get into downloading statements, answering tons of transaction questions, or filling out forms.

- I've given my accountant access to my accounts so they can extract the information they need. When they've got questions, I've told them to figure it out and only come to me if it's vital.

Overall, when you speak to potential partners it's important to state from the start that these are your expectations and requirements. If they can't do all the above, move on to the next partner. There are 20,000 mortgage brokers, 20,000 solicitors, 20,000 accountants, 20,000 letting agents – in other words, tons to choose from! If you also remember my rule about NOT haggling for services, then they'll work out the best way to do everything for you.

Remember the target – become an anonymous landlord. Ignore the costs for the time being, as long as your property is profitable, it's great! It takes balls and bravery to stick with the above mentality. It takes discipline not to say things like, "Leave it with me", "I'll just do it myself", or "It'll be quicker if I just get it done."

Replace those phrases with "Who can do this for me?" – stick to that. Keep your time for yourself, your kids, partner, mum, dad, dog – whoever you want to spend time with. That's why we invest our cash – for more time to spend with the ones we love – not for a second job helping out mortgage advisers, solicitors, agents, and accountants!

LET GO OF THE FEAR OF BEING RIPPED OFF

There can be a suspicion among some landlords that contractors and other people they work with are trying to "rip them off" (as I mentioned in Chapter 6 in relation to letting agents). While I acknowledge that this can be a problem, you won't ever become an anonymous landlord if you suspect that everyone you work with might be trying to rip you off.

Also, if a contractor is going to rip you off then it doesn't matter if you're there managing every part of the project or not, you're going to get ripped off. I've seen examples of this in both instances. However, there are some great ways to identify the good contractors, as I've mentioned.

People have asked me why I tell my contractors what my budget for a refurbishment is – their question is that, surely by saying I've allowed £15,000, that contractor will tell me that it'll cost £15,000, even if they could do it for £14,000? Yes, that may well be true, but if you think like this then my question to you is, "So what?". Also, I'd like you to think of this another way, because I think sharing the refurbishment budget will actually achieve more for your money. Let me explain ...

If you're treating your property investing like a business, then you will map out your budget for each project before you get started. You'll have a spreadsheet detailing the purchase price, your costs associated with the purchase, and the budget for the refurbishment. Let's put that into figures:

Purchase price: £100,000

Costs associated: £10,000

Refurbishment budget: £15,000

Total cost of the project: £125,000

You will only go ahead with that project if you know you can afford all of those costs, and if you know that this property will deliver you the return you're looking for even after spending that money. In that case, why does it really matter if a contractor could do the job for £14,000 but instead charges £15,000, as long as that's within your plan? I would argue, in all honesty, that it doesn't. However, I would also argue that a decent contractor would do more for the money.

If you tell your contractor that your refurbishment budget is £15,000, they'll work out a £15,000 refurbishment for you. If you tell them it's a £20,000 budget, they'll work out a £20,000 refurbishment. Having more money available simply means they'll buy more premium materials, fixtures, fittings, furnishings, kitchens, bathrooms, carpets, paint and so on. The point is, if you spend your time worrying about saving £1,000 on a £15,000 refurbishment, you'll never get anywhere! Instead, set your budget and go with that.

There are a few other points I share with landlords who worry about contractors (or other professionals) ripping them off. Firstly, a good contractor is not going to try to rip you off because they will recognise that they can get more business with you in the future if they charge a fair price and do a good job, especially if you inform the contractor that you intend to build a portfolio.

But even if they are overcharging you, as long as it's within your budget, you don't have to worry about it. Your job is to get the project to completion, that's it. Stay in your lane, set up the project, set up the plan and put other people in position to execute that plan for you.

Another observation I've had over the years is that some people seem to hate it when others make a profit from providing a service. If a contractor told me that the materials for a job were going to cost £5,000, the labour would cost £5,000 and that they'd make £5,000 in profit, as long as they aren't going over my £15,000 I'm happy with that.

Some people might think I'm crazy, but my logic is that if my contractors are making a decent profit on my jobs, they will want to do a better job for me and they'll want to keep doing business with me. Imagine how much more service and focus you're going to get if the contractor is making good profit from you. Imagine how quickly they'll try to solve problems, answer the phone, keep you happy, look after you. That's worth a grand, in my opinion.

By trying to shave £100 off here, or £1,000 off there and haggling with contractors over everything, you lose sight of what you're trying to achieve and you damage the bigger picture you're working towards. You want to become an anonymous landlord. To achieve that goal you need people who will work for you, and who will do that work to a high standard without needing to be micromanaged every step of the way. You need people to WANT to work for you.

If you start haggling over every quote, the quality of the work your contractors will produce for you will be lower and none of them will want to go the extra mile for you. You'll get a reputation for being tight and that won't serve you on your journey to becoming an anonymous landlord. In fact, it won't serve you anywhere, at any time. The most successful property investors I know are anonymous landlords.

In my experience, when you develop a strong relationship with a contractor, they will tell you if they can complete a job for below your budget. That's great, but it shouldn't be an expectation. However, if you haggle from the start, that will never happen. Instead they'll likely provide a lower quality of service, will be more likely to cut corners, and they won't prioritise you.

Now, some contractors will agree with your haggled price. However, when the job is coming to completion, you're over a barrel if the contractor needs to charge you more. Remember, the contractor's quote is simple – materials plus labour plus profit. If more needs to be done to the property than initially thought, it's you who will have to cough up the extra money.

WAS IT WORTH HAGGLING?

Mike bought a property to refurbish and keep as a rental. He asked my lettings team to get a quote for the refurb (as we were going to let and manage the property). My contractors quoted £22,000. Keep in mind, you get what you pay for, especially with contractors. Mike took this quote and contacted several other building firms. He then came back to us with the cheapest quote he could find and asked if our contractor would match it. Ours said no.

Mike then did the same with the other contractors until he'd haggled with each of them and got the quote down to £18,000. Nice! £4,000 saving, right? Not so fast ...

The contractor started the work. He'd picked up the keys from my office, already complaining about this "tight arse" customer. Two months later, the job still wasn't done. We went round to inspect the property because my lettings team always visits the property during a refurb to make sure the contractor is also getting it ready and compliant for letting – it was only half done!

The contractor said the refurb had cost more than the initial quote and they needed the owner to pay an extra £6,000 to get it finished. The contractor wasn't ripping Mike off, but things go wrong in refurbs, costs go up and more work can be required. I believe the contractor had every intention of completing the refurb for £18,000 but it doesn't always work like that. I also believe the contractor knew they were quoting to win the job and that they could add more on at the end if they needed to.

As I've said, EVERY investor should allow some money as a contingency. But Mike refused to spend the money. The property stayed empty for an extra few months and eventually Mike had to spend the money anyway to finish the refurb. So, not only did it cost more than the initial quote from our contractors, it also lost him three to four months of rent!

This comes back to your mindset as a landlord and treating property investing like the business it is. What you need are contractors and other professionals who understand the expectations you're setting for them, and who can complete their work to whatever target you set them. You calculated numbers that you were happy with when you planned the project, so why would you be unhappy if a contractor comes back with a quote that aligns perfectly with those figures?

I have no doubt that on many occasions I pay a bit more than I could. I know my solicitor is one of the most expensive solicitors in my area, but I factor their costs into my plan and my calculations so I know they're covered and, because I pay a bit more for their service, my projects get prioritised and I have direct access to my solicitor whenever I need it.

If you've ever bought and sold property, you'll know how tricky it can be at times to get hold of your solicitor directly – I have a mobile number and I know I can call any time I need to. They see me as a high-value, high-priority, repeat client, which means my projects get treated as such. This all makes my life as an anonymous landlord infinitely easier. Again, I didn't get into property investing to take on more work, more responsibility, or take up more time. I got into property to become an anonymous landlord (and also an anonymous investor).

It's the same with my mortgage adviser, my contractors, my sourcing agents/property brokers and all of the other specialists I work with to run and manage my business. Yes, I might pay a little bit more but that's returned by the level of service and attention I get. For me, that's value for money.

FOCUS ON THE BIG PICTURE

The key is to stop focusing on individual costs and to instead look at project costs as a whole. Create an in-depth financial calculation for every project you work on. Input the cost of the purchase, your sourcing agent or property broker, your mortgage adviser, your solicitor, the refurbishment and any other costs associated with the investment to get a clear picture of the overall cost. That's the figure to focus on.

It doesn't matter if an auction house is charging me £7,000; or a solicitor is charging me £250 more than ABC Solicitors down the road; or if my mortgage guy is charging me £200 more than Cheapo Mortgage Brokers next door. All that matters is the investment as a whole and your target to be an anonymous landlord. If that works, it works.

When you have all of this information readily available (and if you pay a fixed rate to your specialists, the majority of these costs won't vary from project to project), it makes it much easier for you to assess whether a specific property is really a good deal. By having a simple spreadsheet that details all of these expenses before I make a property investment, I can make sure that it delivers the returns I need.

That means I don't ever feel the need to haggle over £100 here or £300 there, because I know that, even if I'm paying a little more, I'm still achieving my target and everyone I work with is happy. It's win-win. If you want to create good relationships, everyone must win from them.

What's more, if you haggle over every cost for every project, you're making your life much harder than it needs to be. You'll have to constantly reassess your plans and every project will end up being different. You'll get dragged into the details by necessity and you'll ruin the relationships in the process.

When you haggle over services, all you're doing is deprioritising yourself, because ultimately you're giving yourself more work and taking more time setting up and managing projects than you need to. Keep one eye on the big picture and always ask whether it's worth that extra £200 if it saves you a whole lot of time, energy and hassle. In fact, don't even ask that question. Just focus on the reason you invested in property in the first place, stop being a tight-arse and start building a team of people who want to work with you.

To become an anonymous landlord, you need to put a regimented system in place that you can rely on and trust that if you keep feeding it in the right way, it will keep delivering you similar or the same results each time. The more you tinker with and change that system, the harder it is to predict the outcomes of projects and the harder you're going to have to work to fill up all of your pots of profit.

As I've said before, property is the easiest business in the world and what I've shared with you so far in this book is how you can make it easy.

> "This is how to make property easy. If you constantly change the system, it's not going to be easy."

ANONYMOUS LANDLORD ACTION POINT

Create a spreadsheet to allow you to calculate your overall project costs. If you already have specialists with whom you work regularly and who charge a fixed rate, put these costs in – now you won't need to update those fields unless something changes.

---

9 SPOTTING CHALLENGES AND PROBLEMS

Al drums his fingers on his desk as he idly scrolls through the email from the contractor, Ed. Five hundred pounds to repair a leak in the roof – he's sure he can get it cheaper than that. After all, he thinks, contractors recommended through letting agents often tend to inflate their rates. He reaches for his phone. After two rings, he's greeted with a brisk, "Hello?"

"Mike, hi, it's Al. I've got the rental place on Browning Avenue? There's a leak in the roof that needs repairing. I've had a quote for £500 but if you can beat it then you can have the job."

"Ok, I'm over that way this afternoon, I'll take a look and get back to you."

"Thanks," Al says as he ends the call.

A few hours later, Al's phone rings, "Yep," he answers. "Al, Mike here. I've had a quick look and sure, we can do that for £400 for you."

"Thanks for that Mike, I'll be in touch."

"Sure, no problem." Al purses his lips, then dials a different number.

"Ben, I've got a roof repair job I need you to look at, at my place over on Browning Avenue?"

"Sure, what do you need?"

"It's just a small repair job. I've had a quote for £400, but if you can beat that then the job's yours."

"I'll need to take a look first, but let me see what I can do."

"Thanks, pop over anytime today or tomorrow."

"Will do." Al hangs up and smiles to himself.

As he's leaving the coffee shop the next morning, Americano in hand, Al's phone rings. "Hello."

"Al, it's Ben. I've taken a look at that roofing job and it's a bit tight, but I can do it for £350."

"Great, thanks for coming back to me, I'll be in touch later."

"Sure, speak soon." Al strolls back to his car, climbs into the driver's seat and dials Ed's number.

"Hello, Ed speaking,"

"Ed, hi, it's Al, with the property on Browning Avenue that needs the roof repair. Look, your quote of £500 is a bit too steep. I've got a contractor who can do it for £350 so if you can match it, the job is yours."

"I don't think we can go that low on the quote, but let me get back to you."

"Sure, thanks." He hangs up and then dials Mike.

"Hello."

"Mike, it's Al. I appreciate you sending over your quote yesterday, but I've got another contractor who says he can do it for £350 – if you can match it the job is yours but, if not, I'll have to go with him."

"Mate, I already undercut one quote, if I drop again there will be no money in it for me, I'm out."

"Suit yourself," Al says as he hangs up.

In that scenario, Al has broken all the rules of the anonymous landlord. He's squeezed the contractors to the point where they will make no money from that repair job. The outcome is that he's forced to use the cheapest contractor, who is also likely to do a poor job as a result of the low price they're being paid. It will likely be completed using the cheapest materials and the labour will probably be squeezed in between other jobs to make it financially worth the contractor's while.

Would you do the same with your mechanic? "Please use the cheapest materials and do a rush job". No. He has also upset both the other contractors he uses, which means they'll likely be wary of working with him in the future, or simply refuse to quote for him.

This might not be evident at this stage but you can very quickly gain the "tight-arse" reputation with contractors. The best contractors (the ones you want to work with) won't even bother with you as they've got lots of other customers (because they're so good).

Al has also damaged his relationship with the letting agent who sent the original contractor to quote, because his behaviour has undermined their relationship with their contractor. The outcome is that the letting agent tells Al that, in future, either he agrees that when a tenant requests a repair their contractor will handle it, or he can do it himself.

Now imagine that Al has five properties and that he now has to source quotes and manage the repairs on all of them. That's a lot more time and energy on his side, all for the sake of saving £50 here or £100 there.

HAGGLING NEVER PAYS ...

I have a landlord with four properties in my letting agency who insisted on my lettings management team contacting him every time a repair or maintenance job was reported by his tenants. In one case, there was a leak. He asked my team to send our contractor to the property to give him a quote. He'd then take our quote and go round to other contractors haggling the price. The landlord sent the cheap contractor to fix the problem.

The tenant reported the same problem again a week later. The landlord went through the same process again. However, this time we insisted that we send our contractor to fix the problem because our contractor refused to spend more time on this landlord's properties without getting paid to do the actual work. The cheap contractor wouldn't answer his phone to this landlord because he was a tight-arse. The landlord reluctantly agreed, the problem was fixed (properly this time) and the landlord paid twice.

In the meantime, my letting agent's contractor wasted his time. My lettings team wasted their time. The landlord wasted his time. The tenant complained three more times because this process took the landlord a couple of days. My lettings business got a bad review from the tenant (this is a true story so you can check the review out for yourself). Who wins here? Do you want to know how much the landlord was trying to save on the £260 quote? £40. Amazing.

Remember why you got into property investing – it wasn't to become a letting agent, a tenancy manager, an administrator or a project manager:

it was to give yourself a stronger financial future and a better quality of life. If you behave like Al, you run the risk of becoming all of those things, however, because you frustrate the people on your team who you need to do those jobs for you and can irreparably damage those relationships.

It can be very easy to slip out of being an anonymous landlord and start getting involved in the day-to-day aspects of landlording that you're trying to leave behind, especially if you start worrying about money or having to pay for expenses you weren't expecting to crop up (like emergency repairs). It's easy to start spending your increased income and relying on that income to support your new lifestyle.

In this chapter, I'm going to explore some of the most common challenges to remaining anonymous that landlords face, and share some solutions that can help ensure you don't get dragged into areas that you want to stay out of.

CHALLENGE: TEMPTATION

As soon as money is involved in any area of your life, many people become irrational or unintentionally greedy. It's just human nature – as soon as most of us have some "extra" money, the question is always, "What can I spend it on?" That applies whether you win £1,000 on the lottery or receive a £500 pay rise – you start thinking about how you will spend it. Very few people automatically think about investing it, especially if it's "only £1000". It doesn't seem enough to invest so you should just think of ways to spend it – holidays, clothes, decorating, Xbox.

It's no different when it comes to property investment, because you will start to see that £500 profit going into your bank account each month and if you give in to temptation you will want to spend that money. You might buy yourself nice things, go on an extra holiday or even just eat out a couple more times each month. All of this adds up and ultimately means you will have longer to go until you achieve your overarching financial goals.

I'm talking from direct experience here. When my property business started making profit, I was ordering more take-aways than I've ever ordered. I booked more trips for me and my family. I bought more clothes. I bought a new set of golf clubs, a golf bag, golf shoes, golf clothes ... yes, I play golf, in case you wondered. I was less disciplined with money. Before I was making good money from my property business, I didn't have a whole lot of money. So every time I had some money I would put it to use, invest it, use it properly. When I had more money, I started being a bit careless with it.

SOLUTION: STICK TO YOUR PLAN

The solution to temptation is rather simple: stick to your plan! Everyone's plan will be different, so you need to, firstly, create your own plan for property investing and then make sure that you follow it, even when there's the lure of a holiday or a nice meal out.

When I realised I was frittering away all the money that I was making from my property business, I made an immediate change. In fact, it wasn't a change: it was simply getting back to my target. I'm building all of this so I can give my children financial stability and security. I'm not building all this so I can make a few extra quid now. I'm doing it so my family has an extra few million quid in the future.

Let's imagine you're starting with £100,000 to invest. You have a ten-year plan whereby you intend to use that £100,000 to invest and reinvest with the aim of creating an income of £5,000 per month. Once you hit that level of income, you can give up work and property investing will become your sole (or certainly main) income stream.

The key is having a goal and a target: your goal is to stop working and live off the income from your property investments, whereas your target (in this example) is to earn £5,000 per month.

The reason temptation is such a huge challenge, and one of the major pitfalls on the road to becoming an anonymous landlord, is that if you start relying on your property income and using that to support your lifestyle now, you're never going to reach the target you've set for yourself within that time frame.

It starts straight away too. You notice an extra £500 each month left in your bank. You spend it once, then you get used to it. When you reach the point where you should have been buying your next property, you've spent half of the cash so now you've got to wait longer before you can buy your next property. Not the end of the world, right? But you've added two years to your plan. For what? A load of nights out or a couple of holidays?

CHALLENGE: THE DOWNWARD SPIRAL OF FAILING TO INVEST

Failing to invest ties in very closely with the previous challenge of giving into temptation, in that spending your property investment income on your lifestyle is often why you don't have the money you want available to invest.

When you started on your property investment journey, however, I'm willing to bet that your intention was to reinvest the money you were making and, in doing so, grow your wealth, improve your financial stability, and ultimately work towards achieving financial freedom.

It is a downward spiral and I would say I see this in around 80 per cent of the people I work with who want to become anonymous landlords. They start relying on the income from their property, rather than accumulating, compounding and investing it. However, this means that as soon as a tenant moves out, they feel the pain of "lost income". All of a sudden they don't have that £500 a month coming in. Or it could be that the property simply requires a few repairs over the course of three to six months, all of which eats into your profit and therefore your short-term income.

Either way, you start to feel the pinch and that makes you start looking for places where you can "save money". You feel as though you need to "do something" to protect this income stream because you're relying on it, and then it's not long before you're self-managing that property. You get dragged into all kinds of areas you'd rather not be involved with and often you don't even save that much money by doing so.

I have an anonymous landlord mentality. I don't rely on my property income at all. I accumulate it, re-invest it, compound it and continue growing my portfolio. That won't change until I hit my target. Set your target, stick to it.

SOLUTION: THINK OF IT LIKE OTHER INVESTMENTS

You have to (and I can't stress this enough) think about your property investment as you would any other investment opportunity. You should never see your property investment as an income (until you've achieved your goal and your target has been met).

You would never invest in Apple or Amazon shares with a view to relying on the income you can get from them each year. You invest in the stock market because you want to put your money into an investment vehicle that can grow over the long term. Property is just another investment vehicle.

Remember property is a business. Just imagine for one moment that a friend of yours who is setting up their own business asks if you'd like to invest in exchange for becoming a shareholder. You say, "Yes", because you feel there is a lot of potential and opportunity. Once you've committed to the investment, you'll hand over your £50,000, hoping that it will grow and in the future it can provide you with a return on investment.

If you are in this situation, are you going to ask the owner of that business to pay you £1,000 a month as a salary from the start? Of course you're not, because you are looking for long-term return on your investment. If your friend's company started making a little bit of profit, say £1,000 per month, you would want them to reinvest that profit in order to continue growing the business. You wouldn't want your friend to stop growing the business so you could take the £1,000 per month profit out. Property investing is the same.

APPROACH YOUR JOURNEY TO BECOMING AN ANONYMOUS LANDLORD WITH DISCIPLINE – HERE'S AN IDEA …

With both of these challenges, there is an element of discipline involved. From day one, you need to see the money you make from your property investment as separate to your spending money. You can't view it as "your money", otherwise you will spend it. It's not your money, it belongs to your target.

One of my top tips to help create this discipline is to make sure you have separate accounts for different purposes and I create automated transfers each month. This is helped by the fact that I have a "money day" every single month which is where I check all transactions and accounts. It's something I enjoy doing and I do it for business and personal finances.

For example, I have three personal accounts that I split my income between – my family account, which is where all of my household bills and general living expenses for my family get paid from, as well as whatever we all need to generally enjoy life; my personal spending account, which just receives a small amount each month so that I can pop out for a beer, have a nice dinner out or buy bits for myself if I want to; and my investment account, which is the money I have to invest each month.

When my income gets split, my investment account is the first one that gets paid. It's normally 50 per cent of all my income and I have a set amount that is transferred from my income into my investment account every month. I do this without fail. Then I invest it. Sometimes it's property, sometimes it's the stock market, sometimes it's crypto, sometimes it's other investments. One way or another, I invest it. Relentlessly.

The point is that I know what my income is each month and I separate and allocate it accordingly.

With my property investment business I have two accounts. One is my rent account. This is where all the rent comes in and all the expenditure goes out. This makes life so much easier for my accountant. It's a dedicated account for property income and expenditure.

The second account is my tax account. Every month I transfer 25 per cent of my profit to the tax account to make sure I've got enough to pay my tax. I learned this the hard way some time ago when I would be doing OK with money and then I'd get hit by a tax bill which seemed to wipe out all of my profits. Take my advice, don't spend your tax money. It's not yours.

But all of this is only possible by being disciplined. This is why it's so important to know both your goal and your financial target for achieving that goal. The key is to make sure you and your family have enough to live and enjoy life, without spending everything you bring in each month.

The more disciplined you can be and the more you can reinvest in your properties, the more quickly you'll see the returns you are looking for. The best part about being disciplined is that you can automate and systemise it. For example, set up standing orders to allocate your money automatically. Check your personal and business income and expenditure each month and adjust as you need to.

What you are aiming to achieve is compounding returns. Let's come back to our example of a landlord who wants to have an income of £5,000 per month from their properties to enable them to give up work. The following chart shows how your returns compound.

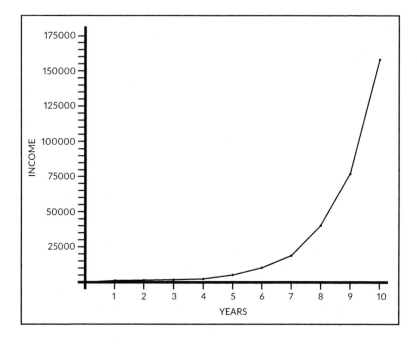

The difference between good investors and bad ones usually shows up in those early years, when you have got an additional £600 or so coming in and you decide to spend some of it. Instead of leaving all £600 in your property investment, you take out £300 a month for one year, so you've slowed down your growth curve.

However, once you've done this the first time, it gets easier and easier to do it again, until, before you know it, at the end of the year you haven't saved enough to invest in your next property.

That also means that your returns in the following year are lower and therefore that you continue to move more slowly up that curve, because you only have one property instead of two. Let's imagine that by year three, you're only just buying your second property instead of your third, which was your original plan. Now your ten-year plan has become a 20-year plan because you fell behind in those early days.

Always come back to your plan before you start taking extra money out of your property business. If, right now, you earn £5,000 per month and your plan is to replace that income with £5,000 per month from a property portfolio, you need to focus on achieving that goal before you start paying yourself any extra.

I'm only seeing the real effects of compounding now that my income is growing and I'm reinvesting rapidly. It's quite exciting!

CHALLENGE: PASSING ON RISING COSTS

A ten-year plan like this is all well and good, but of course your outgoings are not going to stay the same forever. Mortgage interest rates can go up, or new legislation can be introduced that will require you to spend money to comply with it as a landlord. Your own personal expenditure can change too.

Let's take mortgage rates as an example (which is a very timely one as I'm writing this). If you have a property that you rent for £1,000 per month and your expenses for that property are £500 per month, you're making £500 each month, which you've calculated is what you need to earn to stay on course with your plan. However, mortgage interest rates have gone up and now your mortgage is costing you an additional £100 per month.

To stay on course, that means you will need to pass on that £100 increase to your tenants, which can be very hard to do. Many landlords absorb these rising costs themselves because they have "good tenants" in their property and don't want to upset them. However, it's essential to view your property as a business and, just like any other business, you need to maintain your margins for delivering your product and/or service.

Or, you can try to save the £100 in other ways. It's vital not to stop being an anonymous landlord here. You could also consider that, for the short term at least, you might have to revise your initial plan. Plans can adapt and change with the times. No successful business ever stops changing, improving or adapting. Your property business is no different. In extreme times, you might need to take extreme measures.

As I write this, towards the end of 2022, we're seeing major mortgage rate increases. My strategy is to change my portfolio so I am making profit. That's all. I might sell a couple to reduce mortgage balances on some properties to make sure I'm still in profit. Or I might reduce expenditure in other areas. With a portfolio, you have portfolio options with finance, insurance, etc. The target must be profit and to stay profitable. In the short term, you might need to accept a lower profit but remember, this is a long-term investment. Sometimes you'll make more, sometimes you'll make less.

SOLUTION: REMEMBER YOUR TENANT IS A CUSTOMER

I'm not saying that it's an easy decision to increase rent to cover higher costs, but you have to think of the situation slightly differently. Just as your property is a business, that means your tenant is a customer.

Now, if your mortgage payments increase by £100 per month and you don't pass that on to your tenants, you are essentially giving them £100 per month. There is no other business in the world that just gives its customers money like that. OK, you've got to keep the rent at fair market value, that's important; however, you must make sure you stick to that so you are able to look after your investment in extreme times.

The key to maintaining a good relationship with your tenants and being able to charge what you need to in rent is to be honest and open in your communication. Explain that the increase in interest rates has resulted in your mortgage payments increasing by £100, tell them that you won't make any money by increasing their rent, and have an open discussion about the situation.

You could set out a strategy to increase the rent over time. For example, increase it by £50 for six months and another £50 thereafter. It doesn't have to be all now. You need to stick with your plan though. We didn't invest in property as a charity. While we're not going to treat tenants unfairly, we are investors who have used our own cash to invest in order to generate a return on investment. Tenants are welcome to use their cash in the same way if they choose. In fact, everyone is welcome to invest their money to try and make profit.

If you treat your tenants well, they are likely to understand and accept the increase. If, however, your tenants respond with, "That's your problem, not my problem," then they are free to leave. You will find new tenants who are happy to pay the rent that you set to cover all of your costs, as long as it's fair market value.

CHALLENGE: KEEPING UP MAINTENANCE IN THE FACE OF RISING COSTS

There is another crucial point to remember when it comes to increasing (or choosing not to increase) rents in line with rising costs – the less profit you are making from your properties, the less money there is to invest in maintaining the properties in your portfolio.

This will have a knock-on effect on the standard of your rental properties, on the experience your tenants have, and on your ability to charge a fair level of rent in the future. You want to be in a position where you can maintain your properties to a high standard, because this will keep your tenants happy and make it easier to rent your property should they leave. It also makes your property less susceptible to problems in the future if you can fix things quickly and to a high standard.

When you become scared about losing a tenant, or about having those honest conversations and passing on rising costs, you stop treating your property like a business and you slip further away from the mindset of an anonymous landlord.

SOLUTION: START WITH PROFIT MARGIN

When you are making any decisions about passing rising costs on, you need to start with your profit margin. If you "give" your tenant £100 a month by not increasing their rent, that amounts to £1,200 per year. Look at this from the other side – if your costs are £600 per month, that means you could afford for your property to be empty for two months and still be down by the same amount. Therefore, if your tenant decides to leave when you increase the rent, you have two months to find a new tenant before you have "lost" any money.

I'm not saying you have to be so ruthless and money driven – completely ignoring the emotional part of your brain, because you can still take the emotional side of the equation into consideration – but first and foremost you have to think about your profit margin and what you need to achieve for your plan and to continue to provide a well-maintained property to your tenants. Remember why you invested in property in the first place. For me, it's my kids' money so I won't give their money away.

When you start with profit, it allows you to explore how you can accommodate the emotional part of your decision making. For example, you might look at the numbers and your plan and realise you can still achieve your plan by making a 40 per cent profit margin rather than 50 per cent. In that case, you might be able to increase the rent by just £50 per month this year, and then another £50 next year, which gives your tenant time to adjust and also means you don't fall behind on your plan.

The key is to take a breath and approach your decisions logically. In some cases, such as the significant cost of living crisis we've experienced in the UK in 2022/23, your ten-year plan might need to become an 11-year plan. But this is a decision you should make based on logic and after having crunched the numbers. Don't go straight to your worst-case scenario – namely that if you increase rent your tenants will leave and your property will be empty forever. Instead, consider the various options from a logical standpoint and then apply emotion to find the one that works best for you.

It's important to remember that you need to make a certain amount of profit each month and year if you are going to continue to reinvest in your portfolio and grow your income from your property business. I talked earlier about the compounding effect of returns, but this can also work the other way, so if you continue to make a loss each year (or erode your profit) those losses will compound, taking you further away from your goal.

CHALLENGE: CALCULATING RISK AND AVOIDING EMOTION

Risk calculations also come back to the figures and it's important that you approach them from a logical perspective so that you can make informed decisions. For example, your tenant is currently paying £1,000 per month and they've lived in your property for ten years. Ideally, you need to increase their rent to £1,100 per month to keep pace with rising costs. However, the property is unusual and it was difficult to rent out in the first place.

In this case, you might decide that the risk of the property being empty for months while you find a new tenant is too great, and therefore that you're happy with your profit margin on this property being lower because it keeps your existing tenant in place. This is a perfectly acceptable decision, but notice how it's based on logic, not emotion. It's not about being scared a tenant will leave, but about having weighed up all the risks and associated costs and deciding that, in this instance, it's better not to increase the rent. It's just as important to avoid justifying your reluctance or concern for increasing rent by using inaccurate reasons – meaning, don't make excuses.

SOLUTION: CLEAN COMMUNICATION WITH YOUR TENANTS

Whatever decision you come to around increasing (or not increasing) rents, clean and clear communication with your tenants is a must. As I explained earlier, most tenants will understand that prices rise and that this will have a knock-on effect for their rent. Some won't, but you can't sacrifice yourself to protect the feelings of others.

As I've also mentioned, you can find ways to soften the challenge for your tenants and blend logic and emotion. For example, you might explain the increase in your costs to your tenant and tell them that you won't increase their rent for the next 12 months, but that it will go up by £50 per month after that point.

In doing so, not only are you giving yourself security in knowing that your profit margins will return in a year, but you are also giving your tenant time to prepare for the increase in their costs, therefore minimising the risk of them choosing to move elsewhere. If the rent is going up anyway, your tenant will hopefully feel an element of respect for you because you've tried to make it work for them too.

CHALLENGE: GETTING A BAD TENANT

Firstly, 95 per cent of tenants are good tenants, which means while you might sometimes be scared of losing "good tenants", there are plenty more good tenants out there looking for homes to rent. However, that doesn't help you if you get one of the five per cent who are bad tenants.

It can be very difficult to spot a bad tenant at the outset, because I would estimate that at least half of bad tenants only become "bad" tenants due to a change in their circumstances, such as job loss, which you (and they!) couldn't foresee when they first rented your property. "Bad" for a landlord means any tenant that makes your life a lot more challenging – such as by not paying rent for a long period of time, or causing damage to your property – it doesn't mean they are bad people. However, the challenge to a landlord of not receiving rent, damage to the property or having to go through a terrible eviction process is very serious, very expensive and very stressful.

SOLUTION: DUE DILIGENCE

While it can be difficult to work out whether someone will be a good or bad tenant, conducting thorough due diligence can help. On a practical level, this includes looking at a prospective tenant's employment status, income, expenditure, previous references and credit check. That is all standard information for you to gather as a landlord.

It is harder to judge a prospective tenant's personality and nature, but you can get a general idea of whether they are going to be pleasant to deal with. I'm not saying you have to like them or want to be their friends, but if their references and credit check all come back clean, and then you meet them and think they are the kind of person who will keep their head down and pay their rent on time, go ahead. If, on the other hand, you meet them and they are rude, you have to ask yourself whether you want to have them as a customer for potentially years to come.

If a tenant is generally difficult, argumentative and unpleasant from the start, there is a high chance they'll be like that thereafter. That's not to say they won't pay the rent every month but I've worked with tenants who pass all the criteria but were quite difficult throughout the referencing and vetting process. Those difficult tenants have always been the ones who have made access difficult for gas safety inspections, agent inspections, maintenance work, etc.

In my opinion a bad tenant isn't just someone who doesn't pay their rent, it's someone who is a bad customer and who is difficult to deal with.

MY RUN-IN WITH A BAD TENANT

I've dealt with plenty of bad tenants in my time, but the first one who springs to mind is a guy we'll call Neil. He was a tenant I inherited when I bought the property he was renting and he was known for being something of a tough guy.

There was a leak in his sink so my team sent a contractor round to fix it. The contractor fixed the leak and then left Neil his phone number, telling him that if the leak continued, or there were any further problems, to call him and he'd be straight round. A couple of days later, the contractor received a call from Neil, who accused him of screwing up his kitchen and threatened to kill him and his family.

Understandably, the contractor contacted us and told us he was terrified. One of my team called Neil and told him that he couldn't behave like that, at which point Neil started threatening that member of staff and the rest of my team. Then he started threatening my company, telling me he'd smash the windows at our premises, beat up my team, and so on.

Now, when you first met Neil you wouldn't have known he'd behave like this. He comes across as tough, but still just a regular guy. Obviously his behaviour was completely unacceptable and we even called the police at one stage. They told us they knew of Neil from his younger days and that he was dangerous, especially when he'd had a drink.

As a result of Neil's behaviour, my entire team refused to deal with him. The contractor, who was our main gas safety engineer, refused to go to his property again so we had to bring in another gas safety engineer to complete the annual gas safety inspection which is required by law. When the new gas safety engineer got to the property, Neil wouldn't let him in. He called us and told us that if we sent anyone to his property he'd "hammer them".

In the end, we had to evict him, which was a terrifying process in itself. We had to involve the police and I had to take measures to protect my business and my team. This is a very extreme example, but I would imagine that most landlords would be more scared of this kind of situation than of having a tenant who couldn't afford their rent.

DEALING WITH AGGRESSIVE TENANTS

If this kind of situation scares you, then I would say that the first way to avoid it completely is to become an anonymous landlord. It won't be you who has to deal with that tenant directly, it will go through your team. That said, you still need to know how to handle an aggressive tenant at your business, and you need to support your team when you do so. This is a risk of being a property investor. Unfortunately, some people are just aggressive by nature and we cannot control that.

In the example I just shared, we started by trying to talk to the tenant and show support for him. When we realised he was being very aggressive, we called the police, which I think deterred the tenant from escalating. But we also made sure we kept him away from me as the landlord. The team tried to talk to him again in a professional manner and continued to treat him with professionalism throughout while maintaining the focus on the target.

We also made sure we accumulated all the evidence that we were trying to access the property to perform a gas safety inspection and that it was the tenant who was preventing this from happening. Finally, we went through the eviction process from start to finish, which is another minefield! I'll cover that another time.

We followed the eviction process in the right way and I was being updated throughout the process but, because I'm an anonymous landlord, I had no direct dealing with this whatsoever. My company brought in a law firm to carry out the eviction to ensure that it was conducted legally and in the right way.

We did all of this because we know what to do after managing hundreds of properties. The law firm knew what to do because they've dealt with hundreds of eviction cases. Eventually, a bailiff was sent round, the tenant was evicted, and we were able to relet the property. This keeps it from becoming personal, thereby protecting you and the people who work for you. Overall, I had nothing to do with any of this as a landlord. Who would want to deal with this?!

THE IMPORTANCE OF MINDSET

This example brings us back to the importance of developing the mindset of an anonymous landlord. If you are going to run your property investments as a business, with all of the right people in place to deal with any problems or challenges that arise, you can't see them as emotional issues, or personal problems.

Each one is simply a problem, and every problem has a solution. In fact, a problem is nothing more than an incomplete task. Focus on finding the solution and then putting a process in place to make sure it doesn't happen again OR it's fixed without you.

Finding solutions involves asking the right questions. By focusing on finding the solution, rather than on the problem itself, you can remove the emotion from it because all the emotion is in the problem. When you focus on the solution, you engage your logical brain and will come to a solution more easily.

This is what an anonymous landlord has to do – solve the problems as they come up without getting emotionally involved in them. Then you can set up your operation to ensure the problems are managed for you. When you have the right team around you, it becomes even easier to find solutions because you will have experts who can advise you and steer your thinking. In some cases, you won't even hear about the problems, because your team will simply find the solution and action it.

You need to empower your team to take action. A true anonymous landlord will tell their team that, if a problem can be solved for less than your monthly profit, they should just go ahead and do it. You don't need to give your approval, you don't need to know about it, and you don't need to get involved. The amount you are happy for them to spend should be based on the amount of profit you take from your property.

When a solution costs more than the profit you're taking from a property, you will need to approve it, but that doesn't mean you have to find the solution. It will simply mean that your team has come up with what they believe is the best solution and presented it to you. This is problem solving as an anonymous landlord.

If you want to get really clever, when there is a repair or maintenance job that will cost more than your rent, you can ask your management team or your partners to spread it over two months. If you've done everything I've said in this book and you've created a good team on trust and relationship, they'll be happy to do this. Then you don't have to get involved, you don't have to make unusual payments, you don't have to think about it. Of course, this is a very rare occurrence but just try to remember the quote: "If it's got to be done, get it done," Tom Soane, 2022.

"As an anonymous landlord, you will always have problems, but you also always have solutions. The key is to focus on the solution and remove the emotion."

ANONYMOUS LANDLORD ACTION POINT

Write a ten-year plan for your property investments – what do you want them to bring you in the long term? Once you know what you're aiming for, you can work backwards so that you know exactly what you need to do to stay on target.

---

10 WHAT HAPPENS NEXT?

We've covered a lot of ground in the previous nine chapters and while a lot of what I've shared is not difficult to act on, it does take time and effort to put what you need in place and get your property business off the ground. You might be right at the start of your journey and not even have your first buy-to-let property yet, or you might already be a landlord who wants to take their property business to the next level. Naturally, your next steps will be different depending on which of these broad categories you fall into.

In this chapter, I'm going to talk about what happens next and give you a blueprint of how you can become an anonymous landlord in either scenario, starting with the new landlord who wants to buy their first property.

THE ANONYMOUS LANDLORD BLUEPRINT: FOR THE FIRST-TIME BUY-TO-LET BUYER

SET YOUR TARGET

Before you even start looking for properties to buy, you need to set your target, which is really important. Personally, I believe there are three phases to your target:

1. **FINANCIAL FREEDOM:** this is the monetary figure you need to achieve on a monthly basis that will allow you to stop work or achieve financial security. This goal will become your first target. My first target was to

earn £3,000 per month from property, because that gave me financial security and I knew that, if everything else went wrong, I could fall back on my properties and this income.

2. **LIFE FREEDOM:** this is the amount you need for freedom of life and to never have to worry about money. This figure will be what you need to feel as though you always have enough. (That said, there is no such thing as "freedom" because we all have our problems and worries – life is a series of problems and your success is defined by how well you overcome those problems). I set my life freedom goal at £10,000 per month from property.

3. **DREAM FREEDOM:** this is how much you need if you want to live your dream, whether that's buying a yacht, travelling the world or getting a top-of-the-range Rolls – Royce. I set my dream freedom goal at £83,000 per month from property. This target is the one that will likely change as you advance along your journey as an anonymous landlord, because the more success you have, the more you'll reassess what's possible and start setting that bar higher and higher.

The reason starting with your target is so important is that doing so enables you to build a plan that will deliver that target. Many people start at the beginning by buying a property and when they make enough money they buy their next property and so on. But what you actually need to do is start with the end in mind (your target) and work backwards.

Let's say that your financial freedom target is to make £2,000 per month from property. Now you know that, you can work backwards to calculate how many properties you need and how much each of those properties needs to make to allow you to earn that £2,000 per month. Once you know that, you have a much clearer idea of the kinds of properties you need to invest in, as well as what you'll need to do each year to scale up your property business.

When you calculate this, try to include about eight per cent of the rent which will generally be allocated for maintenance. That isn't a rule, it's just what I do. This covers most (sometimes all) of the maintenance and repairs at the property. If your target is £2,000 income from property, you will need, for example, four properties bringing you £500 each. This might take you four years and during that time you might need to accumulate the rent profit, refinance to withdraw as much of the growth as you can, and then reinvest. I have an awesome spreadsheet which shows me when and how I can achieve these targets but you can work it out yourself too.

Only once you've achieved your financial freedom target can you start planning for your life freedom target. Once you achieve that, you turn your attention to your dream freedom target – this is supposed to be a constantly moving target, one that drives you to keep investing because you're trying to live out your wildest dreams.

DO IT SCARED

You are going to be scared of jumping into property investment. You are investing, so you are going to be terrified that you'll buy a property, it will all go wrong and you'll lose all of your money. So many property investors won't realise they're scared. So many property investors won't accept they're scared. But fear comes in many forms. Worry, nerves, concern, apprehension, reluctance. There is one thing fear is not: weakness.

Whenever I've talked to property investors, the ones who have achieved success are the ones who accept their fear. The ones who never succeed are the ones who are too proud to accept their fear. But when you're investing, losing money is always a risk, because there is no guaranteed money when it comes to any investment. If you spend all of your time looking for a guaranteed return, you'll never invest because there is no such thing.

So, you have to invest even though you're scared and you have to accept that you're going to be scared. However, it's also important to remember (as I explained in Chapter 6) that what you're scared of is exceptionally unlikely to come to pass. It's all in your mind and when we're scared, our brains work in worst-case scenarios.

If the property market crashes, how much will it really crash by? Will it crash to the point that property is worth nothing? I think it's safe to say the answer to that question is no! If your tenant doesn't pay rent, how long will it take to evict them? Yes, you might take a hit in the short term in that instance, but you won't be stuck with a tenant who doesn't pay rent forever.

It might take six to eight months to evict them which means you'll need to cover your costs for that time. In a lot of cases you can also get that debt back too. In other cases, you'll have a decent landlord insurance policy or, if you work with my company, I might have guaranteed your rent for you whether the tenant pays or not. This is called my VIP service and other agents might offer this too. It's worth asking!

The human brain tends to focus on the worst-case scenario, which, funnily enough, is *created* by your brain. But when you think about it logically, that worst-case scenario is never going to happen. Having said that, it's worth having the right protection and contingencies in place to minimise risk.

You might be scared, but feel your fear, understand it, accept it and do it anyway. Buy a property and get started. It will probably be a workhorse rather than a unicorn, but that's good, because there will always be a market for workhorse properties, so if you do need to sell then it won't be difficult. Remember that buying an investment property doesn't mean you will be stuck with it for the rest of your life – if it's not working for you, sell it. "Start now, get perfect later," – Rob Moore.

There will always be a reason to not buy a particular property, but as I explained in Part 2, an anonymous landlord focuses on the reasons to buy instead. Come back to the PRESS test – is the property profitable, reliable, easy, simple and safe? If yes, then make the purchase.

My top tip for alleviating your fears around buying your first investment property is to make a list of every fear you have, and then put a monetary figure next to each one of how much it will actually cost you if it happens. Your list might include a property market crash, a tenant not paying rent, or something going wrong at the property. Completing this exercise can help alleviate your fears and allow you to buy that first property! When you turn your worst-case scenario into a monetary figure, it's not so scary and you can plan for it.

BUILD A SOLID BASE OF PROPERTIES

When you're setting your life freedom and dream freedom targets, it can be easy to get excited, but to have any chance of achieving these you need to make sure you have your basics covered. This starts by building a solid base of properties that you can always fall back on. These are your workhorses – they might not be the most profitable properties out there, but they will always rent out and you can always sell them if you need to. They meet the PRESS test.

I believe you need to have a strong portfolio of these kinds of properties, before you start moving into the high-profit, high-risk strategies such as homes under multiple occupation (HMOs) and serviced accommodation or short lets, developments, conversions, and so on.

I see too many people chasing unicorns from day one, and getting burned as a result. If your fear is that you will lose all of your investment, then don't plough it into a high-risk property at the start. I've seen people who have chosen to invest in an HMO that will make £1,000 per month, rather than investing in a PRESS property that will give them £400–£500 per month.

It's easy to see how temptation can get the better of you in that instance, but an HMO is a high-risk investment and sadly I've also seen people put their money into these kinds of property and then lose it all.

To put this another way – if I offered you a 90 per cent chance of making a ten per cent return, or a ten per cent chance of making a 90 per cent return, which deal would you take?

If you build a solid base of properties from the beginning, you will always have that base to fall back on. It means you can go ahead with some more adventurous, high-risk investments if you want and if they go wrong, you have your solid base to rely on.

A NOTE ON HMOS

If you buy correctly when it comes to HMOs, then you can do very well. However, they are much riskier property investments for a number of reasons and they can appear so attractive to the untrained eye. Firstly, you need more tenants to fill an HMO and the tenants you do have will tend to change more quickly. Often people don't live in an HMO for more than a year to 18 months. The tenants you get in HMOs are also less likely to look after the property.

As a result, you'll often have much higher maintenance and repair costs for an HMO than other properties and you'll find you will need to refurbish more often. In addition, because there is a high turnover of tenants, you will probably find that each room is empty for at least one month a year and you will need to keep paying a letting agent to keep reletting rooms in the same property.

HMOs are also harder to finance and they are harder to sell, because fewer people want to buy them (and the challenges with obtaining finance also make it harder to find buyers). Mortgage payments on HMOs tend to be higher than on standard properties and insurance costs are considerably more. In addition, you need to budget for licensing and compliance, and trust me when I say there is a great deal of compliance required for HMOs, as well as substantial fines if you fall foul of any of the regulations.

There are a couple of ways to minimise your risk with HMO properties. Firstly, calculate the worst-case scenarios to include reletting, maintenance, refurbishment, empty rooms, increased mortgage rates, increased insurance, increased management, increased legislation. Secondly, look into the demand. HMOs aren't always for students. There are other HMO markets that might want to take your rooms.

Thirdly, larger HMO properties might qualify for commercial finance which could be more lucrative. Fourthly, check the sale market for HMO properties. If there are loads for sale it could mean that there are lots of HMO landlords who are not making enough profit from them. This is a warning not to buy them in that area. Or, it's an indication that you need to make sure your HMO strategy is air-tight before buying.

Overall, the reason an HMO is attractive is because the headline will show you that you can buy a property for £200,000 and rent it out for £2,000 a month as an HMO. This is not always the case. Don't get distracted from your logical due diligence because you see something shiny.

BE REALISTIC ABOUT THE RETURN YOU'RE GETTING

As a general rule, most landlords will make £300–£500 per month on a buy-to-let property (although that is very dependent on the area in which the property is located). In some areas you'll make more profit per month but less in growth. In some areas you'll make less profit per month but more in growth.

But remember that the return you make on a property is relative to the amount of cash working you have in the property, as I explained in Chapter 4. This is why it's so important to calculate the cash yield you'll make on each property investment and to know what a good cash yield is in your area.

It's a common misconception that landlords keep all the rent they receive from their tenants, because in reality they don't, even if there's no mortgage on the property. There are always costs associated with renting a property, from management and insurance to maintenance/repairs and compliance. These costs all come off the rent you receive from your tenants before you see a penny.

In fact, owning multiple properties with mortgages is considerably more profitable than owning fewer properties without mortgages, as I explained in Chapter 6. What's more, by owning more properties, you're mitigating your risk more effectively.

It doesn't really matter how your property makes profit, either through monthly cash flow or growth in value (appreciation). It's all your money. I see it all as different accounts. It doesn't matter if my money is in my current account, equity in my property, stock market account or another account. As long as it's in one of my accounts it's good.

So, if I'm making £5,000 per year in appreciation and I'm making £3,000 a year in rent profit, I'm actually making £8,000 per year in profit. It's all my money. The only difference between money in my equity and money in my bank account is the length of time it takes to withdraw. So it's important to see the whole of your investment and not just the sexy monthly cash flow.

I remember speaking to an investor who bought around 50 properties in the North West. He was getting pretty good cash flow on those but the value wasn't really increasing. He was OK with that at the time. However, he lives in Portsmouth (my home city) and when he came to refinance them all, he was disappointed that he couldn't get much money out because they hadn't really grown in value that much.

He calculated that he'd have got twice as much cash if he'd used the same cash to invest in Portsmouth, simply because the South tends to grow more steadily in value. The moral of the story is that cash flow is awesome but if you're investing long term, appreciation can be so much faster and so much more lucrative.

DON'T FORGET TO FACTOR IN TAX

When you are starting out as a property investor, it's important to consider tax and how much you will pay. There are two main ways in which you can structure your business – you can own properties in your personal name, or you can set up a limited company and own properties through that.

Which option is best for you will depend on your personal circumstances and the size of the portfolio you want to build.

If you opt for the former (buying properties in your name) then the rent you receive will be classed as income and you will be taxed according to the income tax bracket you fall into. You also generally can't claim expenditure back, because this is considered your normal household expenditure. However, the upside is that if you choose this option you won't need to pay the bookkeeping and accountancy fees that you would if you set up a company. You also won't be subject to company laws.

If you set up a limited company, then you only pay corporation tax on your profits, which means you can claim your expenditure back and that is a definite tax relief. However, if you have a limited company you will need to pay people to help you run it, such as accountants, bookkeepers and so on. In addition, mortgage rates tend to be higher for companies than they are for individuals, so this is a further consideration.

My advice is to consider how many properties you'd like to own and what your personal circumstances are. Speak to an accountant or tax adviser. This is the first thing I did – I spoke to my accountant and worked out which route is best for me. If your goal is to build a sizable portfolio of properties, it could well make sense to go down the limited company route.

Similarly, if you are already a higher rate tax payer (or close to being a higher rate tax payer) then you have to consider that the rent from your property investments will be taxed at the 40 per cent rate, which is a large amount to lose each year. However, this might make sense if both your mortgage rates and your costs are lower. You'll find there might not be a big difference. For some people, on the other hand, there is a significant difference.

The key is to work out what tax you will be liable for on any property you are considering buying and if you do this at the start of your journey to becoming an anonymous landlord it means you will eliminate any surprises further down the line. As with the rest of your finances, you simply need to do the calculations so that you can make an informed decision.

BUY YOUR PROPERTY THEN BUILD YOUR TEAM

There is always something you can do instead of buying a property, but you will never become an anonymous landlord if you don't buy a property and get started! A mistake many potential landlords make is that they are searching for "the right" property when there is no such thing. You have to find a PRESS property that delivers a return you are happy with and take the plunge.

I know I've said this a few times now. That's because I see so many people that want to invest in property but never do. They just never get started. This is because of their fears, for some people it's crippling. My advice is to go for it! You're not stuck with the property you buy. You can always sell if something better comes along or you need to exit.

Think of this another way – if you find a property that will give you an eight per cent return on your money, is that more than you'll earn by leaving that cash in the bank for a year? The answer is almost certainly yes. You just have to get in the game.

Even if you find a property that produces a five per cent return on investment, that's still better than your cash sitting in your bank account. OK, it might be higher risk but if you think about it in the long term, your money is more likely to grow over 20 years if it's in a good property investment. You've just got to get started.

Get a five per cent return on investment to start with (obviously more if you can). Start making some profit now. If something better comes along, you can sell and improve. But you can't improve something you don't have. You've got to take step one before you can take step two. Some profit is better than no profit so you might as well make some profit.

I talked in Chapter 7 about finding the right people for your team to enable you to become an anonymous landlord, but you can't start with your team, you have to start with a property. In fact, in the process of buying that first property, you might meet some of the people you want on your team – whether that's an estate agent, a sourcing agent, a mortgage broker, contractor, letting agent or a solicitor.

Buying a property allows you to find people in these areas, work with them and, if they are good, build relationships with them. It's important to get along with the people you add to your team and it's also vital that these people join your vision and your way of working. Otherwise, they won't be good for your team.

For example, my firm of solicitors was great on my first property purchase and I got to personally know the solicitor who worked on my case. When I bought my second property, I used the same solicitor because she knew me. I even sent her a very expensive bottle of Champagne when we completed the purchase. Nobody ever does that for solicitors! Even though a good solicitor is vital to your success in business and in property.

When we completed on my third property, she took me out to lunch. It works both ways. But would I have found this solicitor and known I could trust her if I hadn't just bought a property in the first place? The answer is no. Plus, I got a free lunch out of it!

As soon as you have your first property, you will start meeting the people you need for your team and you can build it up from there. If you rush around trying to find the right team before you have a property to rent and manage you will waste time and energy, not to mention money, in the process. What's more, they might not be the right team for you anyway! You know what, just get the property first.

THE ANONYMOUS LANDLORD BLUEPRINT: FOR THE EXISTING BUY-TO-LET LANDLORD

KNOW WHAT YOU WANT TO ACHIEVE BY BEING A LANDLORD

If you already own one or more buy-to-let properties and you want to become an anonymous landlord, you have to begin by addressing your mindset. Start by coming back to why you became a landlord in the first place. As I said in Chapter 1, I'm 99 per cent sure you didn't buy a property with the intention of becoming a tenancy manager, a letting agent, or an administrator.

You became a landlord because you wanted to invest your cash into property to generate a return on investment. That makes you a property investor, rather than a landlord. In my mind, the traditional landlord is being phased out. The landlord is the person who engages in the activity of lettings management, tenancy management, administration, property management and so on.

The anonymous landlord is the property investor who engages other people in the activity of landlording. I've only kept the name landlord in this because it's what everyone recognises. But this is the crucial mindset shift you need to achieve, and one of the best ways to do that is to remind yourself why you invested in property and perhaps, just as importantly, why you didn't invest in property.

So, ask yourself: what do I want from being a landlord? Do I want to manage tenants, the property itself and keep on top of legislation and compliance, especially with all the major changes and reforms in the private rented sector and legislation we've seen over the last decade? Or do you feel as though you *have* to do all of that even though it's not what you want to do? If it's the latter, as you will now know, you can build a team of people who can do all of that for you.

You don't even have to go into as much detail as I have. Start with getting a good letting agent on board. I promise you, a good letting agent will not cost you a penny. Instead, a good letting agent should find a way to pay for themselves. I'd happily introduce you to a good letting agent in your area. I know quite a few of them in most parts of the country.

If you don't already have targets for your property investing, like those I outlined for new landlords, write some. Set out your financial freedom, life freedom and dream freedom targets and use these to frame your decisions about how you run and manage your property business from now on.

COME BACK TO YOUR POTS OF PROFIT

I can think of very few (if any!) landlords who, at the end of their lives, will wish they'd spent more time managing their property portfolios, dealing with tenants and letting agents, calling up contractors and doing all the admin associated with being a landlord.

However, all too often I meet landlords who see paying someone to manage their properties as a cost that they can "save" by doing it all themselves. Often these same landlords are charging below the market value for their rents, and they're too scared to increase the rent in case their tenant leaves.

In addition, these landlords often aren't fully compliant, aren't practising the right standards and, most of the time, they are decent, well-meaning people who don't know what they don't know until they know they don't know it. Most of the time, you only find out what you don't know when it's too late.

Personally, although there might be a financial cost to property management, I see the overall outcome as a saving (and so will any other anonymous landlord). Firstly, if I'm paying a company to manage my property, they will ensure I am always charging the optimal rent, so if it needs to go up it will. Secondly, if someone else is managing my property then I don't have to, which removes all the stress and hassle from the process.

Come back to the pots of profit that I talked about in Chapter 1. If you are filling up your money pot, but in the process are depleting your time, energy, mind and family pots, then is it really worth it? Even if you are trading your time rather than money to manage your properties, your time still has a value. Instead of spending £50 a month to have an agent manage your property, you are spending five hours of your time a month to manage the property – is your time worth more than £10 an hour to you? What else could you do with that five hours if you got it back?

Could you spend more time with your kids? Catch up with friends, your wife, your mum, your dad, your nan? Enjoy some more downtime on your own to improve your mental wellbeing? Play golf? You need to make sure you balance all of your pots of profit, otherwise what's the point?

You also need to think ahead, because if you have ambitions to scale up your property portfolio the amount of time you need to dedicate to managing it will increase as the number of properties does. Of course, if you have the right people in place to manage your properties for you, then the time you need to dedicate to your property investments will remain minimal, regardless of how many properties you end up owning.

When your time on this earth is coming to an end, you will not wish you'd worked more. You'll wish you had more time with your kids, with your mum, your dad, your nan, your wife, your husband, your friends. Create the life you want to look back on: do it now.

FUTURE-PROOF FOR COMPLIANCE

The legislation and regulations that a landlord needs to comply with are increasing all the time and, in the future, compliance could be something that trips existing landlords up. In fact, I guarantee it will be. You can easily see how, if you've had a property for 10 or even 15 years, you became a landlord before there was any significant regulation of the private rental sector. The concepts of landlord licensing, regulations and accreditation weren't even on the radar.

At the time of writing, however, the compliance landscape for landlords has changed significantly. If you've had rental properties for over a decade with no issues, you might feel as though these new accreditations and licences are unnecessary, but regardless of your feelings on the matter, you will need to comply with the regulations.

There are already regulations that you might be falling foul of without even realising it – do you renew your gas safety certificate every year for every one of your properties? Do you carry out an electrical installation condition report every five years? Is your property rated as a minimum of an E for energy efficiency? If it's an HMO, do you have a licence?

Are you complying with the housing health and safety rating system? Have you completed the tenant's right to rent checks every year? Have you followed the correct procedure for chasing rent? Do you know the exact requirements for maintenance and repairs? Access to the property? I could go on for hours, there's so much to follow. But that's why you take on an expert. They live their lives knowing this stuff.

Depending on where in the UK your properties are located, you may already need a licence to operate as a landlord of any kind – this is currently the case in Wales, as well as some parts of the North East. It's safe to assume this is going to become a requirement across the UK.

In addition, there are the recommendations from the Regulation of Property Agents (RoPA) working group to consider. Among the recommendations is that every property managing agent (which means you, if you're a one-man-band landlord who manages their rental properties themselves) needs a specific qualification to be able to operate. Personally I believe this is absolutely fair and the right thing to do for the UK's private rented sector.

Many existing landlords who have previously managed their properties themselves are quite worried about these regulatory reforms, however, because they need to keep on top of them and comply with them.

Contrast this with an anonymous landlord – I have a managing agent taking care of all of my properties. Needing a specific qualification to operate is their concern, rather than mine. Of course, I have to do my due diligence and make sure they have the necessary qualifications, but it is on the managing agent to take the course and become qualified to the required level.

Be honest if the growing regulatory burden has been causing you any level of additional anxiety or stress. If it has, even if it's only raised your stress levels by one per cent, isn't it worth getting someone to manage your property (or properties) for you and, in doing so, protecting yourself?

Essentially in taking steps towards becoming an anonymous landlord, you're future-proofing your property investment business.

THE FOUR CATEGORIES OF LANDLORD

Which of these four categories do you fall under? (Be honest!) And which of these categories would you like to be in?

Landlord #1: is compliant and follows all the legislation, but doesn't provide good customer service. They don't do anything extra to make their tenant comfortable. Their goal is to follow the law and make money – they will be hit hard.

Landlord #2: is the opposite of landlord #1 in that they really take care of their tenants. They are probably charging too little rent and they just want their tenants to be happy. They are non-compliant with at least some of the regulations, but they don't realise they're not fully compliant. It's very expensive for them when they find out.

Landlord #3: is fully compliant and provides a good level of service to their tenants. They are the best of landlord #1 and the best of landlord #2.

Landlord #4: is non-compliant and demonstrates poor practice in terms of looking after their tenants. I'm willing to bet that no one reading this book falls into this category, because these landlords have no interest in improving either their business or the quality of the properties they own.

I wouldn't be writing a good book for landlords if I didn't put some further thoughts on the white paper published by the Department for Levelling Up, Housing & Communities in June 2022[3], which revealed that 30 per cent of private landlords in the UK are like landlord #3, while 24 per cent are like landlord #2, demonstrating good practice with their tenants but mixed compliance. A further 35 per cent of private landlords are like landlord #1, and just 11 per cent are like landlord #4.

BUILD GOOD RELATIONSHIPS WITH CONTRACTORS AND AGENTS

Another interesting statistic from that government white paper, as I mentioned in Chapter 1, is that just 18 per cent of landlords use an agent for management services for their properties. Of that 18 per cent, I would estimate that around one-third aren't anonymous landlords and still get involved in the management of their properties in one way or another.

As I discussed in Chapter 7, to become an anonymous landlord you need to have the right tema around you – or *find the who* to help. You can do this even if you're a landlord with only one property. The key is to build strong relationships with contractors and agents and to put the right agreements in place to empower your contractors to deal with simple or low-cost issues without having to come to you first.

---

3 Department for Levelling Up, Housing & Communities, (2022), *A Fairer Private Rented Sector*, June, available at: https://assets.publishing.service.gov.uk/government/uploads/system/uploads/attachment_data/file/1083378/A_fairer_private_rented_sector_web_accessible.pdf

The main barrier to being able to do this as a landlord with only a small number of properties is building those relationships. As I said in Chapter 7, you should never haggle over the cost of services, especially if you have ambitions of becoming an anonymous landlord. When you treat agents and contractors well, they will be much more inclined to set up long-standing agreements to work with you.

Ultimately, your goal is to become an anonymous landlord and you need to decide how you can achieve that with the management of your properties. I'm talking about the tenancy, compliance and maintenance – everything. These are services you will have to pay for, but come back to your pots of profit and ask yourself whether paying some money for a managing agent will help you top up your time, energy, mind, and friends and family pots.

If there are aspects of managing your property that you genuinely enjoy, by all means keep doing them, but that doesn't mean you can't pay for help with the areas that you enjoy less or are less experienced with. For example, most letting agents will work with you to make sure your property is compliant with all the relevant legislation.

GETTING INTO THE ANONYMOUS LANDLORD MINDSET

All of this leads to the same thing – developing the mindset of an anonymous landlord and property investor. You will think of your time and money differently when you have this mindset.

For example, let's say you get paid £25 per hour in your job. Your car needs cleaning and it's going to take two hours of your time to do a thorough job, or you can pay someone £20 to clean it for you. In the two hours you save by not cleaning your car, you work two hours of overtime and earn £50. Even once you minus the £20 you've paid someone else to clean your car, you are still up by £30.

Come back to your dream – are you envisioning sitting on a beach, cocktail in hand while the money is rolling in? The people who achieve this lifestyle aren't property or tenancy managers, they are people who have property and tenancy managers working for them. They might make ten per cent less profit, but they get 100 per cent of their time. That's the investor mindset.

"This is how an anonymous landlord thinks.
They know the value of their time, they know why they invested in property, and they are clear on what they want to achieve through that investment."

ANONYMOUS LANDLORD ACTION POINT

Take whichever of those blueprints applies to your situation, make a list of each of the steps and work through them. Write down the actions you need to take under each step to allow you to make progress towards becoming the anonymous landlord you want to be. Once you have your actions you know what to do – get on with them!

CONCLUSION: RUNNING AN ANONYMOUS PROPERTY BUSINESS (ALL PLAY NO WORK)

I'm going to finish this book where I started it by asking what are you going to wish you'd had more of when you're at the end of your time? Whatever that answer is for you, whether that's to spend more time with your family, travel more, or have less stress and anxiety, follow that dream.

If you think like this, you won't just become an anonymous landlord, you'll become an anonymous investor. You'll be a present family member and you'll have minimal stress and anxiety because life becomes easier when it's not all on you. Whenever you're in doubt, come back to that thought of what you'll wish you had more of when you're at the end of your days.

This is genuinely how I live my life. Sometimes I fancy doing some work and sometimes I don't. On the days when I don't, I'll go and play golf, or take my kids to the park. One day, while I was writing this book, I decided that I wanted to put together a really awesome talk about how to get from zero to £1 million in your business, and I did that in between my meetings that day.

Why am I telling you this? Because you have to do what you want to do in your life. If you want to become a property investor, invest in property; but whatever you're investing in make sure you set it up so that it's growing and being looked after for you so that you have the space to move onto the next property or investment, or spend more time with your family, or focus on a different side of your business.

Now that I've got my properties, my entire business strategy is that every time I make some money from my business, I put it back into property. I keep repeating this process and, as a result, my property investments keep growing and growing. My property business grows by itself and the more it grows, the faster it grows. The key is setting up your property business so that you're not exchanging your time for money, because that allows you to scale it in a way you never could if you were to remain a DIY landlord.

The reason you've read this book is because you want to break free of being a DIY landlord. You want to top up all of your pots of profit and you want to become an anonymous landlord, just like me.

No matter how few or how many properties you've invested in, trust me when I say that you can become an anonymous landlord. Start by changing your mindset and the rest will follow.

I will happily connect you with my lettings team if you're a landlord who wants to talk about letting and management. Or, if you're thinking of buying an investment property, I'll happily connect you with my property brokers who source buy-to-let investment properties.

You'll need to contact me – tom@soanegroup.co.uk – or find me on all social media platforms.

YOUR ANONYMOUS LANDLORD CHECKLIST

I've pulled all of the action points I've shared at the end of each chapter together into a handy checklist that you can work through on your journey to becoming an anonymous landlord.

- Make a list of the five pots of profit (money, energy, time, mind and family) and give yourself an honest score on how you're performing in each area. Mark yourself out of ten, with ten being the highest and one being the lowest. Which pot (or pots) of profit have you been neglecting?

- Make a list of all the services you provide to your tenants on a monthly and annual basis. Explore each one in turn and assess whether you are providing good customer service for each. Score yourself out of ten for every service and be honest! Where could you improve? How can you make good customer service great?

- Go into whichever property investment groups you're part of on social media platforms and write a post asking for recommendations for sourcing agents and property brokers. You'll be surprised by the response you get!

- Calculate the cash yield for your next investment property, or your most recent property investment if you've purchased one in the last year. Are there any figures you don't have easily to hand? Make a note of what those are, if so. Create your own spreadsheet to save time on the due diligence for your next investment, and to ensure you include all the data you need in your property investment calculations.

- Work through the TOM acronym for your next property investment. Write out your target, objectives and method.

- Do the maths for your next property deal and, if you're considering making a cash purchase, run the figures for buying with a buy-to-let mortgage so that you can compare the two. Come back to the target you set as part of your TOM – which of these options will get you closer to your target more quickly?

- Make a list of all the jobs related to your property (or properties) that you currently do yourself. Go through that list and highlight all of the ones you could easily outsource. Choose just one of those, research local professionals in that area and find the right person to take it off your list. All gone well? Work through your list and remember, sometimes one person can take multiple tasks away from you. It's all about finding the right *who*.

- Create a spreadsheet to allow you to calculate your overall project costs. If you already have specialists who you work with regularly and who charge a fixed rate, put these costs in – now you won't need to update those fields unless something changes.

- Write a ten-year plan for your property investments – what do you want them to bring you in the long term? Once you know what you're aiming for, you can work backwards so that you know exactly what you need to do to stay on target.

- Take whichever of the anonymous landlord blueprints from Chapter 10 that apply to your situation, make a list of each of the steps and work through them. Write down the actions you need to take under each step to allow you to make progress to becoming the anonymous landlord you want to be. Once you have your actions you know what to do – get on with them!

Scan the QR code below for access to additional resources, tools and guides that can help you become an anonymous landlord and live the life you dream of.

ABOUT THE AUTHOR

Tom Soane is a property entrepreneur, owner of The Soane Group, and host of *The Anonymous Landlord Podcast*. The Soane Group includes Soane Lettings, Soane Properties, Soane Money, Soane Works and Soane Academy. Tom is a public speaker, often talking about property investing, landlording and business, to investor and landlord audiences as well as business owners.

He was inspired to grow his business as a property entrepreneur when he realised how many landlords in the UK go it alone, and run into all kinds of challenges as a result. He could see people needed help to make their property investments truly work for them, and he wanted to provide it.

Having become an anonymous landlord himself, Tom wanted to share his experience with others to not only help more property investors break free of landlording, but also to improve the service tenants across the country receive in the private rented sector.

Tom wants everyone to know that, no matter where they're starting from, building a successful property investment business is achievable! He speaks from experience, having gone from having bailiffs at his door to building a million-pound business operation that works and grows without him.

He has no plans to stop there either! Tom's next target? To build a portfolio of 250 properties and a £10,000,000 business!

Business aside, Tom is the father of two incredible boys, and husband to an incredible woman. "They are my why: they're why I built all this."

Printed in Great Britain
by Amazon

40206503R00145